MW00978333

Be Your Own Hero

Annie Mayfield

authorHOUSE®

AuthorHouse™
1663 Liberty Drive
Bloomington, IN 47403
www.authorhouse.com
Phone: 1 (800) 839-8640

© 2018 Annie Mayfield. All rights reserved.

No part of this book may be reproduced, stored in a retrieval system, or transmitted by any means without the written permission of the author.

Published by AuthorHouse 06/20/2019

ISBN: 978-1-7283-1661-1 (sc)
ISBN: 978-1-7283-1660-4 (hc)
ISBN: 978-1-7283-1665-9 (e)

Library of Congress Control Number: 2019908291

Print information available on the last page.

Any people depicted in stock imagery provided by Getty Images are models, and such images are being used for illustrative purposes only.
Certain stock imagery © Getty Images.

This book is printed on acid-free paper.

Because of the dynamic nature of the Internet, any web addresses or links contained in this book may have changed since publication and may no longer be valid. The views expressed in this work are solely those of the author and do not necessarily reflect the views of the publisher, and the publisher hereby disclaims any responsibility for them.

CONTENTS

SAY HELLO TO YOUR BEST YOU

You have always been you—the you that carries out your day-to-day decisions, the you that holds your heart, the you that keeps all your secrets and knows absolutely everything about yourself. However, it is time to be your *best* you—the you who is capable of becoming your own rock star, your own dream turned into reality, your own hero.

When we look at legendary icons—Steve Jobs, Oprah, Nelson Mandela, Martin Luther King Jr.—we think, *Well, of course they were who they were or are who they are. I mean, they were just born that way, right?* No. All of these people have something in common: they realized the door to success swings *inward*.

This book takes you through a series of life-affirming essays that give you granular practices and perspectives on how to combat the daily physical, mental, and emotional struggles living today imposes on us. With social media and societal standards on how to think, act, look, and be everywhere, it can be easy to lose sight of who you truly are and what makes you happy. This book capitalizes on the idea that in order to live your best life, you must become your best you. You'll find that by reading this book, you will have the tactics and tools to intentionally live each and every day by design in order to save yourself from yourself.

Negative self-talk and the effects it can have on how others and the world perceive you is a central theme of this book. This theme aims to educate younger men and women that we can create ourselves to be whoever we wish to be simply based on the way we talk to ourselves. We choose which thoughts to project to the world through our actions, and it is our actions that mold us into the people we become. We have the pen in our hands to write the script of whoever we want to be. Greatness is not a genetic predisposition but instead an accumulation of habits, skills, and rituals practiced and acquired over time. If you can choose to think the more helpful thought (note here I did not say positive thought but helpful thought), you will find that you can launch yourself into this world as exactly who you wish to be, not who society deems you to be.

I am your ordinary gal. I'm a regular junior in college, your classic twenty-year-old worrying about my body, zits, grades, boyfriends, boy friends, girls, and my family. Something I can say with my full heart and soul, though, is that anyone can be legendary if they do the interior work. Neither your age, your background, whether you're in college or never went to college, nor even your current circumstances matter. What matters is how you choose to live the rest of your moments, who you choose to show up as—your own victim or your own hero.

This book is intended to light that spark in you that shows the opportunity you have each and every day to put on your hero cape and save your own damn self. No one has to do it for you, and in fact no one truly can. Only you can pull yourself out of your own poor habits, poor decisions, and poor circumstances. The beauty in that, though, is once you do, you realize you have a power that is richer than anything money or fortune can offer: the power to shape your own destiny.

CHAPTER 1

Be Your Own Second Chance

I was coming back from SAT tutoring. It was around ten o'clock at night, and all I could think about was how exhausted I was. I had just sat through a three hour SAT tutoring course … and even though I was all for getting a decent grade to go do the whole college thing, every time I drove back from that tear-provoking room, the only thing going through my mind was how I would do anything and everything possible not to go back to that soul-crushing, spirit-sucking vortex of multiple choice practice tests, true or false questionnaires, and word problems that left my brain feeling as if it had just run a marathon at Usain Bolt speed while spinning in circles—at the same time.

I was sixteen. I was so cool because I had my cousin's old beat-up Ford Explorer given to me as a crowning jewel of passing the driver's test. I called it the Hulk. I'll tell you, though: I didn't expect to get my license the first time I took the test. Most people were banking on me not getting it that day, especially after I knocked down not just one but every single cone on the parallel parking section. That was after I showed up in the wrong shoes (apparently flip-flops are not driving test attire) and had to resort to the only other footwear in my trunk, my alligator Stompeez Slippers. Every time I hit the brake, the mouth would pop open ready to chomp. After I got the passing grade (by God's saving grace), every time I drove, I did that thing where I propped my left leg up in the seat (saw a girl do it in a movie once) and let my right hand take control of the steering wheel with my Pandora Hottest Country Hits radio blaring. Like I said, I was *so* cool.

This particular night was pouring down rain. I wasn't allowed to take the highway yet. I'd only had my license for a little over three weeks, and my overprotective yet extremely loving dad wasn't ready to let me drive on the highway. Of course, as any sixteen-year-old daughter would do, I drove on the highway every single time getting to and from SAT tutoring. I loved how soothing the highway was at night; there was hardly any traffic (a rare luxury in the heart of Atlanta), just me, the Hulk, and my Dierks Bentley. On this night, like every other night, I turned onto 285, turned up my radio, and was ready for my therapeutic time spent on the smooth lanes of the highway headed back home.

It happened so fast. When people ask me to try and recount it, it's almost as if it was all a blur. People ask if I was scared, if I was freaking out during it, and I can honestly say I don't even remember.

Maroon 5's "Misery" was playing over the speakers. I was singing along. I was trying to get in the lane next to me, closer to the median, because that's where the faster traffic was going. I turned my blinker on and was switching lanes when the glass shattered. That part is still vivid to me now, four years later. I can still hear the Hulk's glass shattering in the back as it simultaneously started swerving and flipping over the four lanes of oncoming traffic.

From an outsider looking in it was hell in real life. It was a scene of complete destruction—the depiction of someone in a big green Ford Explorer meeting the kiss of death. My car landed on its left side in the grassy median. The first thing I thought—amid the shattered glass and the chaos of the *Oh my God, what just happened?* in my brain—wasn't that I needed to call the police or my parents or even that I needed to get out. It was *I need to turn the volume of my music down! I don't want the person who gets me out of here to think I'm* that *into Maroon 5!* Y'all, I kid you not. That was my first move: turn the dang volume down to hide my Maroon 5 obsession.

Glass was in my hair, the car was destroyed, and I was lying on the driver's side window. I will never forget this man, who seemed to me like an angel at the time, crawling up on the car to open the passenger-side door, which now faced the sky, and hauling me out.

Back on solid ground, safe, and hardly scratched, I sobbed. Not your pretty girl, reality TV, airbrushed, "makeup perfect yet still crying" type of sobs. I mean your ugly, puffy-faced, eyes swollen, cheeks red, full-out hyena-sounding sobs. I couldn't believe what had just happened. I got into a car wreck. *Me.* This is supposed to happen to people on TV shows and in movies and in the news but not to me.

Who do I even call? I didn't even know where to start. Do I call my best friend? My boyfriend at the time? My parents, even though I wasn't supposed to drive on the highway?

I called my mom. My beautiful, selfless, full-of-love mother. By the time the whole fam (I am one of four) got there and emerged from the car, I had been holding it in pretty well. I wouldn't say I was keeping it together amazingly, but any poker face I had completely dropped when my mom wrapped me in her arms. I absolutely lost it.

I don't think I'll ever forget the look on my dad's face. While I was too scared to even call him to tell him I got into a wreck and flipped over four lanes of oncoming traffic, simply because I thought he'd be mad at me for driving on the highway, his face when he held me flashed absolute disbelief. He had almost lost his daughter that night—his sixteen-year-old, tennis player, runner, goofball, smartass of a daughter Annie May, almost gone within seconds.

I don't have kids. But the look on my dad's face that night, on the side of the highway, with ambulance and police lights blinding our eyes, struck a chord in me of the depths of a parent's love for their children that I will never forget.

I remember swerving. I remember flipping. I remember feeling calm. I wasn't freaked out. I didn't think I was going to die, yet at the same time I didn't think I was going to live. I felt a stillness that I hadn't ever felt before, and I don't think I've felt it since. It was a stillness of absolute, entire release. I released whatever I had to the universe. "God, here we go"—that's what I was saying to myself out loud, repeatedly as the car flipped. Looking back, I don't know what made me want to say that or how it came to mind. I don't even really know what it means, to be honest. It just meant that whatever was coming—death, a life filled with injuries or disabilities, a new life of appreciation—I was ready for it. God, here we go.

In life you are going to have moments that feel like a second chance—a second chance to look at life a different way, with a newfound appreciation and a new sparkle. It doesn't have to be a big monumental moment like a car accident, an illness, or a death; it can be what meets the eye as a subtle change—going to a new school, moving to a different town, falling in love with a new hobby, boy, or girl. In fact, I don't believe there are only second chances in life. I think that there are countless chances to embrace a new lifestyle, lead a new path, or embark on a new journey, so long as you choose to look at it in that way.

After my car accident, honestly, not a lot changed (besides me being terrified of changing lanes for a while and my boyfriend of almost a year and a half breaking up with me a few days later; that was rough). Now this probably isn't how you thought this story was supposed to go, but I'm going to be real here for a second. I didn't wake up the next day wanting to prance through the valleys in the sunshine, kiss the flowers, and hug every animal that came into my presence. Oh, heck no. I didn't wake up the next morning feeling as though I'd been wasting my life away and now that I've got a second chance I need to go hug every stranger and sprinkle fairy dust everywhere I go because *God gave me a second chance, everyone! I must be important or something!* Radical life change over here!

Absolutely freaking not. It wasn't at all like that. If anything, it made me question more. It made me feel more unresolved than content and grateful.

I remember waking up the next day, after having to go to the hospital at 4:00 a.m. because even though I said I was fine, my parents insisted on getting doctors to look at me for some type of brain blood leakage, concussion, or whatever they could find. They would never admit this, but I'm pretty sure my parents wanted the doctors to find something wrong with me, simply because after what they had seen, it was easier to accept that there was some damage done rather than sit with the disbelief that I came out without a scratch after flipping over four lanes of oncoming 285 Atlanta traffic.

I looked in the mirror when I woke up, and I was just ... confused. *Why did I not die? Why me? What does this mean? Do I have to go and like end world hunger now? Or cure cancer? What do I do with this? Um—hello, God, this is a lot of pressure here!*

That's the thing about second chances or just being given another chance in general: they only mean the meaning that *you* give to them. They only hold the value that you hold them to have. They could hold no meaning to your life and not affect anything you do. You could have your dearest family member die, but this moment, this opportunity to get another chance at seeing how precious life is, this second chance could mean nothing to you unless you decide to see it in that way. You could move to another state and start a new school or job. This second chance could be the opportunity to integrate more gratitude into your everyday routine, finally start that workout place you said you wanted to routinely do, start cooking more, actually get an online dating app and go on some dates—if you let it.

The concrete acts of moving to a new city, getting into a car accident, getting a divorce or going through a breakup, taking on a new job, or starting a new relationship are not what changes us. They are not what makes us grow. They are not what forces us to take on second chances. Instead, it is our reaction to a situation and how we proceed afterward that enables us to grow and to change. What you learned from the experience, what it taught you, the new life it inspires you to live—thinking of those things after the event and building the daily habit of living out helpful principles are what causes change and the beauty of second chances.

I did not seize the second chance in this situation. I was in a car accident—a situation where my life was just about gone in a poof of an instant. Yet, if you asked me at the time which hurt me more, my car accident where I almost died as a sixteen-year-old barely having lived her life or my boyfriend of a year and a half breaking up with me two days later, hands down I would've said my boyfriend breaking up with me. In fact after that happened, I did not let the car accident act as the second chance for my life that it could have been. I did not see it as an opportunity to instill major change into my life.

God gave me a wakeup call. Here was a chance to go through an experience where I could choose to come out of it looking at life a different way, in a more appreciative, precious, and grateful way than I had been. I could have begun to remind myself every day that life isn't about Instagram likes, how many other girls like my boyfriend, having the best figure or the best highlighted hair, or even (and forgive me for saying this) the more than a hundred likes on your profile picture!

Instead of coming out of that car accident and choosing to look at life in a new light with a new posture of gratitude for the small things—such as the fact I am upright and can walk, talk, and breathe—I didn't even acknowledge it. I forgot about it and continued my high school career living in the superficiality of cartilage piercings, ring-covered fingers, neck chokers, New Balance tennis shoes, laptop cases covered with Mountain High stickers, rolled uniform skirts, and Wallabees.

Something big and traumatic doesn't have to be your big second chance at life. It wasn't for me. It could've been, if I had seen it that way and taken the opportunity to change my perspective on life, but I didn't.

You can be your own next chance. God is always presenting opportunities in our life for us to redirect the way we are living if we are not happy, and you want to know what those opportunities are? When we get up every morning, our eyes open, breath fills our lungs, and a beat stirs our heart. Every single morning is an opportunity for a second chance to redirect your path, your life, fulfill *your* own damn destiny. If something super traumatic or life-altering comes along and changes the way you look at life forever, causing you to live in your state of flow and bliss each day—awesome. Take advantage of the opportunity, and seize it. Set your intentions. Take that second chance.

If not? Awesome! Every morning is a second chance to set a new tone for your life. How do *you* want to live? How do *you* want to be perceived? How do *you* want to love, to learn, to shape the world, and to leave your mark?

Which leads to the other thing about second chances. I don't believe we get just one second chance. I think any and every moment we intentionally mark out to be another opportunity to better our lives is a second chance. And there are millions of moments over the course of a lifetime—meaning there are millions of chances to start over, try again, or begin something new.

My car accident, though it was an incredible opportunity from God for me to alter my life and start appreciating it more, wasn't my second chance because I didn't live it out to be that. I went right back to my old habits three days after the accident. I was sixteen when that happened, so it might have been my immaturity at the time that meant I couldn't recognize an opportunity to act on a wakeup call on my life when I got one. However, I think most of it had to do with my fear. I liked my life, not because it was extravagant or because I was all that happy, but simply because *I was comfortable.* Too many times people are more likely to stay in their unfulfilling but familiar circumstances than to take a chance on finding a happier, more satisfying life simply because the path to get there starts in unknown territory. As a twenty-year-old writing this, I can tell you that no second chance is a second chance if you don't live it out to be that. Any moment can be a do-over, or *any* moment can be a continuation of the same ways you have always lived your life. You must decide if you want to live your life in your unsatisfying comfort zone or take the leap toward something better yet unfamiliar.

Every day you get a second chance to live the life you want. Every day is a clean slate, a fresh start. What can I get excited about today? That is how I start every day to give myself another chance at being happy that day.

You can be your own damn second chance. You don't need external circumstances—an alien from the sky landing on your lawn and telling you how precious life is, a fortune teller revealing your future, a car accident, a fire, or an illness—to decide when and how you can start living your life again. Be your own wakeup call. Be your own second chance, each and every day. Set intentions, and live out the life that, if for some reason your life were on the line in this very moment, you could say you're proud to have lived.

TAKE NOTE:

1. Life is not a calculated algorithm you can manipulate to get a particular outcome or result. To take chances means to jump into uncertainty. Remember, though, that on the other side of that leap, regardless of whether you get the result you initially desired, you will *always* grow, and that in itself is the greatest of takeaways.
2. Be more watchful in your day-to-day experiences for any second chances God or the universe is giving you that day. Maybe it is that new person who said hello to you, that new coffee shop calling your name to go work in, or a new gym membership you've been on the verge of acquiring. It could be a car accident, a death in the family, or a huge move from one city to another. Regardless of how big or small you make it out as, *choose* to capitalize on that moment, and use it as leverage to propel your life into the direction you think will lead you to the most prosperity.

Ask, "Is this a person I could see myself learning from a lot? Is this coffee shop somewhere I see myself finding solace and comfort in? Is this city a new place I can explore to grow my experience and sense of adventure? Is this death in the family going to bring me closer to the family I still have with me?" Ask yourself these questions to use any chance you have as a chance to guide yourself to a more prosperous and fulfilling life—the life you've always wished for.

CHAPTER 2

Be Your Own Comparison

Comparison can suck the life out of you. Growing up, I always found this a struggle, especially because the people I compared myself to the most literally lived in my own very house. I have the most amazing siblings. They're either a brainiac wizard, athletic superstar, or a combination of both.

I have three siblings. My older sister, McRae, is one of the most incredible, free-spirited people I've ever met. She's traveled to more than twenty-five countries, lived in both Switzerland and Russia, is an absolute genius, and seems to always be able to "figure it out."

Growing up, she went to the same high school I did; we were even in a class together—honors chemistry. Yuck. I remember one week in that class, and I was absolutely done. We studied together for the first quiz. She made an A+ and I made a C-. That basically sums up the difference in our ability for anything chemistry-related—or school-related, for that matter. To me McRae had something I felt I didn't—brainpower and common sense. I was always comparing my success to her success in the classroom, although it really wasn't even a competition because she blew me out of the water every time. I never felt I could be smart like her or free-spirited enough to just get up and go travel the world, but she could always "figure it out." She has this fiery passion for adventure, tenacity for travel, and desire to excel at whatever she puts her mind to.

Then there's Lizzie, my younger sister. This girl is a freaking athletic rock star. She plays soccer at West Virginia University and has always been a gifted athlete but also worked her ass off to get the opportunities she's gotten. For soccer, the recruiting process takes place a lot earlier than tennis, so Lizzie and I (even though she was only a sophomore and I was a senior in high school) were going through the recruitment process at the same time. Now let me just say, this sucked. Majorly *sucked*. I was constantly comparing myself to her and my offers to her offers. Thing was, I was not nearly the class of tennis player that Lizzie was as a soccer player. I would never be able to look at the schools Lizzie was looking at to play because I would never be able to play there. While Lizzie looked at huge universities like Georgia, West Virginia, Auburn, Alabama, and Tennessee, I was barely expecting to be able to play tennis at a small D1 school. Most of the schools I was looking at were D3 schools or super small D1 schools, like Wofford which has a little under fifteen hundred students.

I constantly diminished my own capabilities and my worth because to me they didn't measure up to Lizzie's. To me I wasn't as good, as athletic, as worthy, or as valuable. Comparing myself to her every single day nearly destroyed me. Thing was, I was also so incredibly proud of her; I just internally self-destructed because of the thoughts I chose to think, believe, and act on.

That's what I did not realize at the time. Every single thought I was letting flow through my mind either built up my life story or destroyed it. Our thoughts dictate our beliefs, which direct our actions, which produce the outcome of our life, regardless of whatever circumstances may be presenting themselves to us at the time. That is how people amid horrible conditions and situations can still bring themselves to have a smile on their face each day: they have learned to control and generate gratitude among their thoughts in all situations. At the time when I was comparing myself constantly to my sister, I did not realize the never-ending tape being played in my head that said "You will never be as good, as smart, as pretty, or as athletic as she is." I failed to understand that I had control over what this tape in my head played to me, but I chose to let it project negative statements into my belief system instead of helpful ones.

It wasn't just my two out-of-this-world incredible sisters I seemed to compare myself to; my little baby brother was always someone who held a rock star standard. He to me is one of the most gifted people on this planet. He's an incredible lacrosse player and is currently looking to play in college (he's only a junior in high school right now), but that isn't the way

I always compared myself to him. He was so freaking well rounded, it was almost annoying. You know those people I am talking about, the people who seemed to be naturally incredibly at just everything. You study hours for a test, they study the morning of, and you both get the same grade, or they get a higher grade. These are the people who can show up to an interview and knock it out of the park with little to no preparation; they always seem to excel on any field, court, or pool because of their gift of natural athleticism, and they always seem to have an invite to all the parties or plans with friends because socializing is just second nature to them.

Yeah, one of those annoying, incredible people is my brother. He is athletic as can be (over six feet tall and able to pick up any sport he wants) and a genius wizard in the classroom *and* carries a booming social life with more friends than I think I've accumulated in my entire lifetime. He has endless special talents and yet is still humble. I don't even think he realizes how many amazing gifts he has. I always compared myself to the amount of things he's good at. Anything, anything at all—making friends, any sport, any subject—James Mayfield could do it and do it well if he applied himself. I was over there feeling as if I was drowning, dedicating myself to just one area, while James juggled them all and seemed to do it with effortless success.

Comparison will rob you of all joy. This is what it did to me in high school. It tore me up from the inside out and made me feel I was never good enough, no matter what I did. Even if whatever I had done at some point met my standards or even exceeded my expectations, if I saw one of my siblings or anyone in my life really do something even better than what I had done, suddenly my achievement wasn't good enough, and I wasn't good enough. Thing is, there will always be someone who did something you think is greater/ grander/ better than what you have done. If you live in this mentality of comparison, you will always come up short.

Comparison takes another twist for the worse when you throw in today's greatest source for comparison—social media. It is no longer simply the people we interact with in our day-to-day lives that we can compare ourselves to, but now, more easily than ever, we can look into the life highlights of people *we don't even know* just to compare and conclude how much better they are than us.

In a world where Instagram likes are our crack, year-long relationships can be stirred by "sliding into someone's DMs," and photo after photo on the feed constantly reminds us we're not the prettiest, skinniest, fittest, happiest, funniest girl or guy on the planet, and everyone's life is *so* much better than ours—it's easy to feel like absolute crap. It's easy to get stuck in that scroll hole, analyzing picture after picture, selfie after selfie. How does that girl get abs like that? Do you think she works out a ton, or is it genetic? Oh my goodness, this girl has way cuter clothes than me—and look at her boyfriend! I need to get a cute boyfriend like that! Holy cow, that girl is in such good shape, I could never look like that or do what she does in the gym. That girl goes to all of these fun parties! Gah—she must have such an amazing life, way better than my life over here, where I'm eating rocky road and watching Netflix this Friday.

Aren't I right? Aren't these the comparative thoughts that cycle through your subconscious (and conscious) mind every single time you get on your social media feed, whether it's Instagram, Snapchat, or Twitter? Are these not the thoughts that creep into your heart sparking nonstop insecurities day in and day out because you are always aware of how awesome everyone else's life is compared to yours?

Why is it that when someone posts a beach pic of them looking ah-mazing in their bikini, we feel gross about our own selves all of a sudden? C'mon, you know what I'm talking about. When you see your friend or even a stranger post a picture of their perfectly sun-kissed skin, in a tiny little bikini showing off their perfectly sculpted body, you suddenly feel gross. You feel bad about yourself because you saw a picture of someone who is looking smokin' good. All at once you don't feel good enough, simply because you saw a picture of someone you now deem more attractive than you. You don't feel pretty enough, tan enough, or skinny enough; your butt isn't sculpted enough, and your boobs aren't perky enough anymore because you now subconsciously set the standard of "attractive" in your mind as anyone who looks like that girl in that bikini. Since you don't look like her, you're not enough.

If you stop to think about the logic in this pathway of thought, it makes sense. However, it isn't true. It is a lie that our subconscious brain is telling us because it wants to do everything in its power to protect us. Our brains are biologically programmed to make us want to fit in. Thousands of years ago when our ancestors were roaming the earth, if they did not fit in with their tribe, they were expelled. If they were expelled from their tribe, then they were on their own and were headed for death. Our brains don't see fitting in as just a preferable thing to do; they see it as the means of survival. So when you see a girl on Instagram or Snapchat or Facebook or Twitter and set her appearance as the "standard of beauty," your brain is going to automatically make you feel crappy for not fitting in with or meeting that standard.

Break the damn programming! It's time! You, set your own standard. Be your own beautiful. There are so many kinds of beautiful girls out there. You have girls with short hair, long hair, curly hair, and straight hair who are beautiful. You have girls with thighs that touch who are beautiful and girls with big ole gaps in between their thighs who are just as beautiful. You have girls with freckles, girls with glasses, girls with braces, and they are all beautiful. I remember I hated my freckles when I was a little girl. I hated them so bad that when I was at the beach one summer I refused to go out in the sun and sat under the umbrella every single day. The reason I hated my freckles so much was because I had just seen the *Twilight* movie, and Kristen Stewart had absolutely no freckles anywhere to be found on her face. Kristen Stewart was beautiful to me. I wanted to be beautiful like her, so I thought I had to get rid of my freckles to be beautiful.

It wasn't until one day my mom came into my room and was talking to me that I noticed her freckles for the first time. I noticed how mine were just like hers. I have always considered my mother to be one of the most beautiful women I've ever seen, and I'm not just saying that either; people approached me all the time (they still do) to tell me how stunning my mama is. I had never noticed her freckles before, but for the first time I looked at them. I realized that if my mom is beautiful and has freckles, maybe I can be beautiful with freckles too—even if Kristen Stewart doesn't have freckles.

Now what the heck does Kristen Stewart have to do with anything? Absolutely nothing really, except that after learning I didn't have to look just like her to be beautiful, I understood beauty comes in all different forms. Beauty comes in all types of light on all different types of people. Freckles or not, curvy or stick figure, big boobs or little boobs, big nose or small nose ... everyone rocks their own version of beauty.

With social media I've learned one practice that has completely changed my life when it comes to how I feel while scrolling through my feed. I call it the "separate and appreciate" principle. When you see a photo—and you know the type of photo I'm talking about: the photo that causes you to stop mindlessly double-tapping hearts as you scroll; the photo that evokes in you that burn, that anxiety, that heating sensation in your stomach and in your chest where you suddenly don't feel enough; whether it be a girl rocking the perfect bathing suit in a luxurious vacation showing off her perfect bod, or the girl in the cutest romper with the seemingly effortless perfect hairdo at that amazing party you heard about—when you feel that comparative monster in you strike, say the words *separate* and *appreciate*. Separate that photo from your life. Understand that this photo, and the girl's beauty within that photo, has nothing to do with you. Just because she posted a photo looking incredible in her fit, toned body, doesn't all of a sudden make you fat or any less in shape than you were before you saw the photo. Just because she posted a photo of her luxurious trip in New Zealand with the sun hitting her face perfectly and the scenery behind her looking like heaven on earth, doesn't make your life any less interesting or less exotic than it was before you saw her photo.

That's the thing. These photos, these comparisons ... they only have the power that they let them have over us. Separate the photo portraying a snapshot of another girl's life from the life you are living in that moment. They have nothing to do with one another.

And once you do that, you can learn the next part of the principle. Now *appreciate*. Once you've separated the other girl's photo from having any power over how you feel about yourself in that moment, you can appreciate her photo for what it is: a snapshot of something really beautiful or amazing going on in her life at the moment. You're at the beach getting an awesome tan? That's amazing for you! You go, girl! You're traveling the world and just hiked Mount Kilimanjaro? YGG! I could never do that myself, but you're amazing! That's awesome!

Appreciate Instagram photos, Snapchat stories, and Twitter feeds for allowing people to tell the tale of their ventures. But don't let the tale of someone else's day to day experiences make you feel any less about your own life and your own self. They are two separate, unrelated things. Of course look at photos of women for inspiration. Want to get in shape? Heck yeah, follow that girl on Instagram who gives workout and healthy eating ideas. However, don't look at her body and suddenly start hating your own body because you don't look like her.

Separate the photo from your life, and *appreciate* the photo for telling the tale of another bold, badass babe out there showing off her life for the world to see.

TAKE NOTE:

1. There will always be someone who is better than you in your opinion at whatever you feel most confident about. Even if you feel like you're pretty, there is someone prettier. If you feel you are funny, there is someone funnier. If you think you are an amazing football player, there is someone better than you. My point here is not to crush your soul and any self-confidence you have but to encourage you to understand that spending your precious energy trying to be the best at something and getting discouraged when you realize you aren't is energy wasted. The one thing you can be confident in is that no one else in the world does pretty like *you,* does funny like *you*, does football-basketball-baseball-or-volleyball like *you* do it. Only you can do *you.*

2. Social media comparisons—drop 'em. Separate the photo from yourself and appreciate the photo for what it is. It is telling the story of another girl's adventures that have nothing to do with you. Someone who looks rocking in a bikini on an insta pic doesn't make your body any less sexy in a bikini. When you find yourself in the "scroll hole" (subconsciously scrolling and comparing yourself to insta pics), realize the thought patterns you are having. Did you get a pit in your stomach when you saw that girl's workout pic from earlier? Did it make you feel pathetic for not hitting the gym today? Separate the photo from your life. That picture has to do with that girl, not you. She had a great workout; good for her. Maybe you'll hit the gym tomorrow, or maybe you won't. Do not let a picture of someone else's life make you feel any less about your own. They are two different, unrelated entities.

3. Unfollow anyone you realize triggers self-loathing in you. If you follow those gym icons for means of motivation, great. Keep

following them. If you are following them and they aren't doing anything to motivate you but instead just make you feel crappy about yourself, unfollow. Go follow someone else you can relate to, who can instill inspiration in you.

CHAPTER 3

Be Your Own Good

There is bad in us, it's true. Bad isn't put aside for just supervillains or terrorists or the guys in rom-coms you see break up with their girlfriend right after her dog died. It's not something that is made up or make believe but a very real thing right inside each and every one of us.

Not all people see it that way. Someone you know might be absolutely the kindest and most loving, soulful, and Jesus-reflecting person you could ever meet in your life. *You* might even be that person. You know who I'm talking about: the one who hesitates before killing the cockroach in their bathroom because it is a living creature and has feelings (you'd best believe I'm slugging my shoe at that thing, first chance I get). But nope, they're not excused; even they have evil inside of them.

That's simply the point of it all. We all have evil thoughts and feelings. We all have times where the first thing that pops into our head *isn't* something we would ever share with anyone else. Thoughts like *Yeah, that lady should really not be wearing those leggings; her body cannot pull those off—but mine totally could* or *I might not have gotten as good a grade, but at least I'm prettier* or *These people are taking so damn long checking out at Walmart, and I've been waiting to check out forever because they've packed their cart full of crappy food that they totally don't need anyways because they're all unhealthy as can be ….* Yeah, I know. We've all had times where our brains have released these deep, dark, hateful thoughts and sometimes they take us by surprise. The scariest times though are when they don't take us by surprise; when they flow right through our brains without any hesitation, and we accept them as they are.

Let me relieve some of the knot that is building up in your stomach reading this because you know that at one time or another (or every day), you have thoughts like these that come into your head, and you catch yourself answering them, *Wow, I'm a really awful person.*

YOU ARE NOT AN AWFUL PERSON! Now let me be very clear because I don't want you thinking that those thoughts are allowed to run freely in your brain for you to think whenever you want. No, those thoughts, that evil in us, is not good. However, I don't believe it can be erased either. It is in us. It is a part of us. We all have evil in us. Yet, more importantly, the contrary is true as well. We all have good in us. Thoughts about how beautifully a person's soul is radiating as they speak of their passion; thoughts about how to effectively lead a group of people to reach their highest potential; feelings of generosity, love, and passion—this is the good in us!

Regardless of what you believe in—God, the Universe, or some higher power out there—whatever that is to you, it put both good and evil in us. Everyday among these thoughts that jumble our minds, every second of every moment we have the option to act on the good or the evil. Let me break it down: No one is innately born to be particularly good or bad. Over the course of our life, we have conditioned our brains and thus our behavior to think and act in certain patterns. The advantage to this is that if your brain is conditioned to acting on the *good* thoughts, then your actions reflect the good in you (a majority of the time). But if over time you repeatedly fall prey to those hateful, harmful, and negative thoughts, causing you to lash out at people or say or do hurtful things you didn't necessarily mean to, you are reacting to the reinforcement of negative behavior directing your life instead of actively choosing how your life is to be directed.

That is why those people, the ones you think are fairy dust in life form, are as perfect as you think they are. They act on only what is good and pure and loving and soulful. They have the evil thoughts too. The judgmental, egotistical, shameful, dirty, and sinful thoughts are not just something that pops into their head every once in a while, but may even fill their minds every single day. They have just mastered choosing to act on the good. They radiate love, positivity, joy, and gratitude not because those are the only thoughts that fill their minds but because those are the only thoughts they choose to fuel their actions from.

It is a choice every single day. Every single day evil thoughts will crowd your mind. You can make faces, sighs, remarks, and judgments behind the overweight family at Walmart taking over an hour to checkout because they bought basically the whole supply of Kraft Mac & Cheese (you can even do that eye-roll thing where you're not going to outright say you're annoyed because you're "way too nice a person for that and don't want to be rude"; yet you most certainly are going to find a way to nonverbally communicate that you are pissed off and totally judging in some way)—or you can stand there and choose to act on the good parts inside of you. Choose to shift your perspective, and dive a little deeper into the situation. Perhaps they can't afford the more nutritious, more wholesome, yet more expensive foods; or perhaps the mom and dad both work full-time jobs and don't have time to make healthy, home-cooked meals, so they have to resort to food that can be prepared quickly and that all the kids like.

You are not a bad person for thinking evil thoughts—and thinking good thoughts does not make you a good person. The kind of person you are all depends on the thoughts you choose to carry into actions.

Choose the good. Be your own good. You can choose to live out the thoughts that inspire, uplift, and motivate others if you choose that. Take that good inside of you, that good we all have, and emphasize it. *Choose it.* Go shine your light with it.

TAKE NOTE:

1. Do not confuse having evil and shameful thoughts with being a bad person. Everyone has these thoughts; remember, the power in who you are is determined by the thoughts you choose to carry into actions.
2. You cannot banish negative thoughts. *They will happen.* When you have a negative thought, remember in order for a thought to be labeled as negative, there must be a positive contrasting thought as well. Think of the more positive, contrasting thought, and choose to act on that. Do not bury your negative thoughts. Recognize

them without judgment, detach them from your identity, and let them go.

3. For all you "I'm just not a positive person" people out there, I get it. I really do. Sometimes the whole "positivity" thing can be taken a little too far and ends in feeling like positive people must drink some sort of magic pixie-dust Kool-Aid every morning that magically turns them happy in any and all situations.

Here is another amazing exercise to try for my "positivity skeptics" out there. Ask yourself if the thought is helpful or not. A thought can be positive and not helpful; a thought can also be negative but helpful. Choose thoughts that are helpful to you in your situation. Does your thinking this girl is taking way too long in line and how incompetent she is help your situation of getting through the line faster at all? Probably not. If that is the case, think about what a more helpful thought to dwell on could be. Perhaps run your brain through your gratitude list for the day, or think about the amazing weekend you have planned. You could even think about how much writing that paper is going to suck but how you are going to handle it. Choose to think about thoughts that will help your situation. They don't necessarily have to be positive thoughts, just thoughts that will gear your situation to a more beneficial outcome for yourself.

CHAPTER 4

Be Your Own Cheerleader

In high school I would get really down on myself, and I mean really down on myself. I remember times where I would freak out on myself for literally no reason. It was almost as if I wanted to make myself feel bad or cry or feel like crap and worthless. In high school I got called stupid a lot. I got called dumb and told I had no common sense.

Now, most of these comments came from the people closest to me, and I thought nothing of it. Despite getting average grades and in fact having a good head on my shoulders with common sense, I believed that I was stupid because time and time again I had heard it from people. Eventually, I talked to myself that way too. I would call myself stupid or idiotic and say things like "You have no common sense at all." I started carrying out my life in that way, and a lot of my actions, thoughts, words, and questions were centered around a base with no common sense because I told myself I had none, so I believed I had none.

One time in particular, during my senior year I had to fill out a form to get access into my email account for my college in the fall. I needed to get access to my email asap because there were tennis forms I had to fill out by the end of the week to be eligible to play at Wofford College in the fall. I ended up filling out the wrong form, getting locked out of my account, and having no access to the tennis forms. I completely melted. I don't think I've ever screamed the words "I am such an idiot" so loud and so repeatedly in my entire life. I cried, sobbed, broke down … let's just say I thought that because of all this my tennis career was over. What I didn't know at the moment was that all I had to do was text my future coach and it would get sorted out.

The thing is, that moment happened all the time. When something bad occurred, I would talk myself down until I literally felt less valuable than that smear of dirt on your shoe. What did this do? It sure as hell didn't help the situation at all; it just made me feel more like crap. But that's what I did. That was how I talked to myself when something went wrong: I always blamed it on *me*. I always said I wasn't smart enough or capable enough or didn't have enough common sense. Thing is, saying these things over and over again led me to actions that carried out those beliefs. I probably made a lot more stupid mistakes than I would have if I hadn't talked myself down to stupidity.

How do you talk to yourself? Probably not a question you get asked very often. We are often asked how we talk to others—our peers, our parents, our teachers, our mentors, our coaches—but do we ever stop to reflect on how we are talking to ourselves?

When you do something clueless—put the remote in the fridge instead of the leftover sandwich you had for lunch, and then spend all day looking for the remote; or scroll through your feed at night and drop your phone flat on your face (yeah, we've all been there)—what are the words you aim at yourself when you realize you've flubbed up a little bit? Are you "jokingly" calling yourself an idiot or stupid or an airhead? Are you "jokingly" saying you'd lose your head if it wasn't attached to your body?

What if it is a more serious situation—for example, you mess up the car directions and drive an extra five hours north of your destination and have to turn around? Or forget your keynote for a huge presentation at school or your job today that are essential to the success of that presentation?

A majority of the time when we are in these situations—jokingly or not—we use derogatory terms to degrade our self-worth. If you build the habit of saying negative things about yourself, even when you are joking, you are training your subconscious to believe this about yourself. You will eventually truly believe you are an airhead or an idiot or would lose your head if it wasn't attached to you. With those beliefs, you have already struck yourself out of the game of reaching your highest potential before you've even gotten a chance to swing. It is so essential to cultivate your mind-set to be its strongest form.

It's time you start to cultivate your mind-set into being an indestructible force of powerful thinking. Instead of wasting time mulling over how much of an idiot you are and how stupid you are, you want the first thing your mind goes to after a mistake to be *How can I fix this? How can I make this even better than it was before?* To do that all starts with your intentionality in the way you talk to yourself. Swap complaining or talking trash to yourself in favor of problem-solving questions. This is not going to be easy and is going to take consistent intentional training to cultivate this problem-solving mind-set; but after every mistake or blunder, ask yourself, "What is the good in this? Sure, I messed up, but how can I make the new situation even better than before?"

You can have a bulletproof mind-set, one that doesn't stop you from reaching your full potential but empowers you to reach the potential you never thought you had. But that all starts with simply the way that you talk to yourself.

Think of someone you always want to cheer on. You always want them to succeed and do well. This could be a daughter, a friend, a sister, a brother, or even a pet. Would you bash them and call them a stupid airhead when they mess up, even over the slightest of things? Probably not. So why on earth are you talking to your brain like that? Treat your brain like that one you are always rooting for, and then root for it. I'm not saying don't push it and motivate it, but do so in a loving way; don't bring it down or tear it apart. Propel it with self-love and respect; this will create a new thinking pattern in your brain that you are capable and more than enough to handle not only the task at hand but whatever obstacles may be thrown your way along the path.

TAKE NOTE:

1. Be intentional with the way you speak to yourself. Do not react to the first emotion that fizzes up inside you when something bad happens, because more often than not those emotions are not helpful and derogatory (anger, frustration, self-pity, irritation, etc.). Instead, condition yourself to see the opportunity in each situation. What can you learn from here? What lesson is hidden under all this frustration?

2. Try talking to yourself as you would someone you care deeply about. Try this for one day. One whole day, talk to yourself (and yes, I mean through your thoughts, people! Unless you like to talk aloud, which is totally cool too) the way you would talk to your best friend, sister, boyfriend, girlfriend, or little brother—someone you want to succeed, thrive, and accomplish all of their goals. If that person messed up a little, would you scream at them the way you do yourself? Probably not. You are the only person guaranteed to be with you for the rest of your life. You cannot escape you, ever, period. So why not make sure your relationship with yourself, which is determined by how you speak to yourself, is the most fruitful, encouraging, and valued relationship in your life?

CHAPTER 5

Be Your Own Permission

I've got to say, I've never been the type of girl that has been able to just freely "be myself" all the time and never care about what anyone thinks. In fact, this was one of my biggest struggles growing up. I constantly thought about who was looking at me, who noticed what I was doing, what people thought of me. I would always get a twang of anxiety as I got up from the lunch table to go refill my apple juice in the cafeteria because *Oh my god every single eye must've been on me.* Yeah, right. At least that's what it felt like.

And God forbid I should ever go to the bathroom alone in case someone walked by when I didn't have a friend walking with me. I was afraid passersby would look at me as if I had no friends. I kid you not, these were the type of things that crowded my mind all through high school. Even walking to lunch alone, if I passed people I mentally was telling them, *No, I'm just meeting my friends there! I have friends, I swear.*

I bet I'm not alone on this one. I bet many of you, whether you want to admit it to yourself or not, are in your head going *Retweet, girl, retweet!* And why is this so relatable? Because it's human nature to feel like we need permission from society to act or look or feel a certain way. The reason this matter of wanting to fit into society is so prevalent in our culture is because it is the way our minds are conditioned to think. Thousands of years ago, if you did not fit in with the tribe, you were kicked out. If you were kicked out and living on your own in the man-versus-wild world back then, you probably didn't make it through the night. So over hundreds and hundreds of years, our brains were programmed to always do their best to fit us into society so we wouldn't get left behind.

The thing is that, deep down, what we ultimately want isn't society's permission to fit in; instead, we crave is society's permission for us to be able to be ourselves. If you ask anyone if they'd rather get to be their truest, purest form of themselves for the rest of their life, or the generic stereotypical prototype of what society thinks a person should be—nine out of ten people will say their truest self. Why? *Because we are miserable acting as something we are not.* The universe did not put special gifts and passions in you for nothing. It gave you these things as a gateway to the path that will lead you to shine your light. If you close that gate, which many people sadly do because they were put down or ridiculed too many times, you end up feeling empty and miserable.

What's truly ironic is that we all are craving someone else's permission for us to be our own self. If you let someone else have the power to give you permission to be your own self and abide by their standards, you will never be your true self. Everyone has different outlooks and views on life. Everyone sees the world through a different lens cultivated by their genetics, past experiences, nurturing, and morals. So if you are seeking permission from someone else to be yourself, you are never going to get to the point of being who you truly are.

I remember the first time I did a live clip of me speaking on my Instagram story. To some of y'all this may not sound like much, but for me I was absolutely petrified. Just imagine it—the girl who was terrified to walk to the bathroom by herself for fear of what others might think was about to do a vlog on her Instagram story where all her friends and many strangers were going to see. "Annie's up to something a little strange." "Did she really just do that?" "Oh my god, she's one of *those* girls now." That was how I expected people to react. To give some context, this was when I was beginning to grow my physical and financial wellness business, and I was really focused on taking leaps of courage to do whatever it took to grow a successful business. All the young entrepreneurs in this biz at the time talked on their Instagram stories as if it was no big deal, almost like second nature. I knew in my gut this was the next hurdle I needed to jump in order to gain more momentum.

So I was running around my grandmama's house before our

Thanksgiving brunch, and I stopped, scrunched my ponytail to make the curls look a little more perky and wiped that sweat out of my eye. Oh yes, one more thing I should mention: when I decide I want to do something, I'm very much the kind of person that does it there and then. I'm not into thinking it through a million more times or the fiasco of preparing for just this many more minutes. I like to just *do it*. So you'd think I'd perhaps want to doll up a little more, right? Oh no. Straight in the middle of my run, sweaty red face and all, I whipped out my phone and did my first speaking engagement on my Instagram story. I remember it was about tips for a healthy Thanksgiving. It wasn't necessarily about giving out this huge content but instead just jumping over that hurdle of doing the thing I wanted to do and felt I needed to do, despite my fears of what others might think.

To tie up the story, my friends were all super supportive (of course some people had those same exact thoughts I thought they would). Still, it was a huge leap for me. Ever since then I committed to doing video blogs on my Instagram story at least once a week, and now I do them like they are my second nature. I truly don't think I would be where I am in my business or writing this book, if I hadn't taken that leap of faith to trust the gut feeling telling me I needed to post the vlog that day and not let the fear of what others might think defeat me.

What are you putting off right now that could be evolutionary for you, your family, your business, or your life simply because you are afraid of what other people are going to think of you? It could be as small as starting to order salads and fuel your body with great nutrition while your friends order burgers and then get mad at you for ordering a salad and making them feel bad. It could be as big as quitting your job to pursue your lifelong dream of being an actress or a singer. Don't let the walls of society block you in from shining your brightest light. Your light will be too bright for some, but don't let them shade it.

Find those who help you shine your light and help you shine even brighter than you could ever shine alone. They are out there, and the best part is that once you start indulging the person the universe truly meant for you to be, you are going to send out the energy that will attract those people that help you become your truest you even more. Send out the energy into the universe that you want to attract. You want to be confident, bold, daring, honest, and truthful? Send out that energy, and not only will you program your brain to become those characteristics, but you will attract the people in this world who embody them already.

So what are you waiting for? Start that business, do that Instagram story, write that book, *go to the bathroom by yourself with your head held high!* Be your truest you; it was literally what you were made for.

TAKE NOTE:

1. People judge your ability to do something based on *their* abilities. Why? Because this is the only thing they know. So if someone believes you are not capable of achieving something, it is because they are grabbing from their own box of insecurities about their ability to achieve that feat and projecting it onto you. Only you know your true capabilities and the potential you have within you to achieve them. Do not listen to the noise and chatter others will bring telling you otherwise. Their opinions have nothing to do with you but everything to do with them.

2. The moment you take off on your dream and start gaining momentum, there will be people trying to pull you back down. This is because when you do the hard work to chase after your dream, you leave people with no excuse for not chasing theirs. An old adage I love is there are two ways to build the tallest building in the town. One is to do the hard work and build it. The other is to tear down all the other buildings in town. Most people unfortunately choose the second option when it comes to dream chasing. Instead of chasing their own dreams, they tear down the dreams of others so they can continue to be slave to their excuses and comfort zone. The permission to be who you want to be lies within you and you alone. Build the tallest building in the town, and do it by lifting yourself up and not tearing others down.

CHAPTER 6

Be Your Own Belief

Who are my Kanye West fans out there? Personally I'm much more of a country music lover, but the guy's got major talent, there's no question. The way Kanye carries himself is very controversial in many regards. Some call him cocky, some call him confident, and some just think he's flat-out bonkers; however, despite all the controversy, there is one thing everyone can absolutely agree on: he has an unshakable belief in himself.

A man once walked into Kanye's house and the very first thing he noticed was a huge poster of Kanye himself hanging on the wall; you see it when you first walk in. He asked Kanye why he had a poster of himself hanging on his wall, and Kanye's reply really nailed the key to Kanye's success. Kanye said that if he doesn't believe in himself, *who would*?

Belief in life is not simply highly encouraged or suggested, but absolutely necessary for high performers and unlocking your greatest potential. If you don't truly believe in your own capabilities and your ability to figure things out, then you will not succeed as much as you would if you truly felt with every ounce of your being that you were capable of achieving whatever it is you align your body, mind, soul, and heart to set out for.

Believing in yourself isn't easy. That's because in order to believe in yourself, you have to take a hard look at yourself. Yes, *you*; not your phone, your Instagram, your Snapchat, your Twitter, your friends, your parents, your siblings or friends … but *you*. You have to take the time to reflect on who you are and who you want to become. The first step to becoming the person you have always dreamed of being is simply believing in the first place that you can become that person.

Psychology and self-development studies are starting to show that there is no such thing as a genetic predisposition for becoming great or legendary. People who have these legendary titles do not have some molecule in their brains that releases the "greatness" hormone for their success. Instead, they cultivate greatness by the way they live their everyday lives and their belief in themselves.

How do you build belief in yourself? That seems to be the question on everyone's mind. "Sure, Annie, I would totally believe in myself, if I could." If only it were so easy to just flip a switch and have belief start pouring in, right? Belief all stems from confidence, and confidence all starts with consistent daily habits. When you start doing the do, you start building the belief. What happens to most ordinary people is that they create schedules or hold themselves to new standards that they ultimately keep breaking time and time again. After these same patterns keep happening, their brain is wired to think they cannot successfully accomplish any of the goals they set out for, and their belief diminishes or vanishes.

So my advice for you is to create small, daily habits that push you but are realistic for you to accomplish. Do them each day as if your life depended on them. Do them as if your identity is encompassed in these habits. Now I'm not saying you should start going to the gym seven days a week if you've never worked out a day in your life. Start smaller, maybe two days a week, and then build up. If you are someone whose goal is to eat healthier, but you're coming off a straight Zaxby's, Waffle House, and Papa John's diet or a non–calorie-conscious diet, then maybe aiming to eat a salad for every meal and only twelve hundred calories a day is not a realistic goal.

Start not necessarily by counting calories but by aiming to fill your plate up entirely with healthy options when you eat. Or aim to replace one meal a day with a healthy shake or salad. The point is that once you start implementing small, daily habits and consistently holding yourself to them, you will begin to see just how successful you really can be if you put your mind to it. This will exponentially grow your belief in yourself and your ability to do what you set out to accomplish.

Once you put on this cloak of self-belief, it is amazing how much you attract people of the same caliber—people who believe in themselves, are comfortable with themselves, and love themselves. Being surrounded by these people will further your ability to love yourself and realize that you are capable of whatever you set your heart to.

I've always been a huge workout freak. Some use the term obsessed; I prefer the word driven or committed. However, the reason I love working out is the way it makes me feel and the person it turns me into. I feel my best after I've worked out, and the contrary is true as well: I feel my worst when I haven't worked out. I'm not as patient, I get grumpy, I get terse and short, and I just don't feel good on the inside.

I've been in situations before where if I wanted to make my workout happen, I had to make it happen. This might mean leaving the hotel at 6:00 a.m. before my tennis team's match at ten, even when I wasn't in the lineup. I had to make sure I woke up early enough to run my set mileage for the day beforehand. What I've learned time and time again is that if it means enough to you, you will figure it out. No ifs, ands, or buts, you will make it happen.

My confidence does not stem from some innate genetic molecule in me that oozes confidence whenever I tell it to. Nor does Serena Williams's confidence or even President Trump's. It is something that we create moment to moment. Confidence stems from our belief in our ability to figure all things out, regardless of restrictions, obstacles, or circumstances. No matter what is thrown at you, *you will figure it out, damn it!* You will find a way if it means enough to you.

When I embraced this fully, that I was able to "figure it out," my anxiety decreased. Less and less have I worried ahead of time about how I would get my workout in, where I would do it, etc., simply because I came to truly believe that no matter what, I will figure it out because it means enough to me. That strength of "figuring it out" gives me confidence and fuels me.

The other key to upping your confidence and thus belief in yourself is to acknowledge your strength. My beautiful, loving, amazing, badass friend, hear me when I say, "*You are the incredible. You have been through brokenness. You have seen tragedy.* Do not for one second convince yourself that whatever you've been through isn't as bad as someone else's or that you haven't lived a life that's been challenging in some way." Don't get me wrong; some people's circumstances are severely more challenging than others' in a certain point of time, but that does not mean that every person on this earth isn't struggling with something or hasn't gone through something before.

Acknowledge the strength you have been granted through those tough situations. You just had a baby and survived? *Strength*. You just passed your chem test and didn't have an anxiety attack when you had no idea of the answer to the fifty-point essay question? *Strength*. One of your dearest friends just passed away, and you were at that funeral even though all you wanted was to go as far away as you could from seeing your friend's body lying there in the lifeless dirt? *Strength*. You guys all have something beautiful and special within you that has been cultivated through the situations the universe has given to you.

Strength. You have it. Confidence—it stems from the strength you've accumulated through the situations that you've experienced in your lifetime. Belief is what confidence all adds up to. Recognize all the strengths you have inside of you! Don't be afraid to feel strong and worthy and valuable! Because you freaking are! You have gotten through some tough things, guys!

You are here. You made it. You are breathing this very second and reading while absorbing knowledge simultaneously. *Strength*. The fact you picked up this book and are pursuing progress and your self-development is strength. Recognize that, and let it be the foundation of your confidence and your self-belief. It is time to stop downgrading all the incredible things you've done and have gotten through in your life. You are a badass. You are incredible. You can be your own hero.

Why do I know this? Look back at your life; you've done it over and over, time and time again. Whether you've realized it or not, you have saved yourself in every situation. Let that build you up and shine out of you like beams in the brightest sunset you've ever seen. Those beams are your confidence. That whole sunset is your self-belief.

TAKE NOTE:

1. Strength is found in the experiences that make up our everyday lives; look for it, and integrate it into your identity. You have been

and are now going through things that make you a much stronger person than you realize.

2. Don't belittle your strength due to the assumption that others have been or are now going through much more than you. Everyone's battles look different and require different skill sets to overcome. If you put your focus on the significance of someone else's battle, you are losing the fight in your own battle and thus losing the reward of winning it—the strength accumulated from the experience.

3. Belief comes from your ability to always figure it out. You don't have to know right now how you're going to figure it out in the moment, but be reassured that no matter what, when the time comes and you've got to hit pedal to the metal, you will figure out a way to succeed if it means enough to you.

4. Remind yourself of this when you are struggling to find confidence in a situation. Remind yourself that no matter what, you will find a way to happiness and success. Say this to yourself in the mirror, look into your eyes, and repeat it over and over again until you really feel a shift in the momentum you are carrying.

5. Make what I like to call an "I'm a star" list. You know how in elementary school they would give you a golden star for doing something kind and caring to condition your young self to keep doing it? Do that for you now. Not in the same way, unless you want to give yourself a golden star sticker, then totally go for it! But I want you to write down ten stars on a piece of paper, and next to each one write something you are proud of yourself for accomplishing. More often than not there are things you have done that you totally forgot about that were actually pretty major! Did you give birth to a human? Major. Did you survive fifth-period calculus class? Huge. Did you give a presentation on a topic you knew nothing about and had no time to practice for until five minutes beforehand? Definitely star-worthy. Write these down! Remind yourself of your greatness and accomplishments. This will build back your confidence with each achievement you jot down.

CHAPTER 7

Be Your Own Zest

Zest (*noun*):

1. Great enthusiasm and energy
2. The outer colored part of the peel of a citrus fruit, used as flavoring

Got any lemon fans up in here? I swear there's nothing better than a really cold glass of water with some lemons in it. Something about the lemons just makes the whole experience more refreshing and enjoyable. The lemons add a little extra sparkle to the drink. Even though I'm a huge fan of adding lemons to my drink, I know a lot of people who are just plain water people. They don't like the extra sparkle in their water and prefer it plain. Does this mean I should stop adding lemons to my water? Well, heck no. I like it, don't I? I like the extra sparkle, sweetness, and the *zest* that it gives. Would you stop putting lemons in your water just because some other people thought adding lemons made it all "too much" or "too overbearing"? Probably not.

So why is it in the real world when we ourselves are categorized as acting in a way that is "too much" or "too overbearing," we tone it down? We cross ourselves off and conform to the way everyone else does things. Why is it that we stop putting the lemons in our water and block our opportunity to experience the zest?

My whole life I've been known as one big ball of energy. I get the whole "calm down" notion a lot—simply because my energy is always just on fire. I move, I bounce, and I dance (a lot), usually coupled with singing or rapping some song. I'm always wanting to talk to people and learn their names and where they're from. When I was playing junior tournaments growing up, my opponents would get irritated with me because I would try to talk to them during the changeovers (water breaks) in between games when we would switch sides of the courts. I just had all this energy pouring out of me, and I wanted to go explode it all over the world.

A couple years ago I read an article on the difference between thermostats and thermometers. Thermometers simply reflect a temperature that is already set. They do not add anything to the temperature or change it in any way, but merely reflect an existing condition. They do not decide for themselves what temperature they would like to register and have no control over how they are perceived by the people around them; they just mold to whatever environment they are in. Thermostats, on the other hand, set a temperature. They are responsible for exactly the temperature they put out for the other people to feel and decide exactly what environment is going to be created because of them. They do not reflect what has already been predetermined by something else but instead make their own atmosphere.

I'll be the first to say it. You guys, we live in a world of thermometers. And no, I don't mean the physical kind that you find in dorm rooms and in nurses' offices for them to check their sick patient's temperature; I mean, figuratively speaking, about 95 percent of the people on this earth are living out a thermometer life. They simply reflect whatever environment they are in instead of cultivating their own. Their energy matches whatever energy the people around them (family, crowd, staff, congregation, etc.) are putting out, instead of determining what kind of energy they want to personally create.

The 5 percent of people who have really excelled in life—and I mean really excelled: the professional athletes, the millionaires, billionaires, CEOs—understand that in order to be truly successful in whatever they do, they must cultivate their own energy in whatever environment they are in. They spend intentional time visualizing situations they may encounter and how they want to carry themselves and the energy they project and attract.

The key is for this energy to be predetermined. If you go into the day reacting to whatever comes your way and basing how you feel on the circumstances around you, your energy will be just that, a reaction to your situation, thus making it fleeting and conditional. Proactive and predefined energy is a commitment you make before the day starts, with all the potential awaiting you. The true icons of our time and times before us realized this, visualized the potential situations they could experience that day, and determined the energy they were loyal to carrying before their innate reactions had a chance to act. They do not match the energy around them but instead get very clear on the type of energy they want to give and want to receive—and then do just that.

When I was younger, I didn't like having so much energy. I was afraid I would annoy people, especially in the mornings. I am *such* a morning person. I get up at 4:15 and have the same ritual: read my daily devotion, journal for twenty minutes, and then go work out. The mornings literally light my soul on fire, and I just want to go and shine light to everyone, everywhere. To me it represents the mark of a brand-new day and a brand-new opportunity to love people, spread joy to people, and do things that can make a huge impact.

The problem is that not everyone is a morning person. In fact, I think it's safe to say *most* people on this planet are not morning people, and the thought of getting up at 5:00 a.m. is about as bad to them as sticking pins in their eyes. Thing is, when I was younger, I used to conform and act "tired" in the mornings so I wouldn't annoy people. In high school I would tame the bounce, the dancing, the energy, the smiles ... all so that people wouldn't be overwhelmed by my zest or my energy.

Through this I realized that if I acted as if I had no energy in the mornings, I attracted people who had no energy in the mornings. The more I did this, the more I fell out of alignment with who I was and what my soul craved—shining love on everyone in the mornings like one big old dance party filled with energy! In college was when I really started to recognize that if I am true to who I am and start giving off the energy that I have in my heart, then the energy I will receive from people will be aligned with my own energy. I started getting back into my bouncy spirits in the mornings. Five a.m.? No biggie! I'm still going to be smiling ear to ear and screaming at you, "Good morning, sunshine! It's a great day to have a great day!" Why? Because that is *who I am*. I am energy! I am zest! And once you identify the type of energetic person you are or want to be and the type of energy you want to receive from people, you will start receiving that from the universe.

Don't be the freaking thermometer. Be the thermostat! Set your own energy temperature, you guys! Are you someone who thrives off of cooler, chiller energy vibes? Awesome. Embody that, and release it into your everyday interactions with people. Are you someone like me who thrives off of fiery, lit-up, firecracker explosions of energy vibes? Fantastic. Act on that. You will attract the energy you put out into this universe.

Every single day we have transitional moments. This occurs whenever we get out of our car and go into the house, get off the phone and start studying, wake up from a nap and head to our workout, and within that workout switch from cardio to weights ... the list could go on and on. Anytime our focus shifts from one thing to the next or we immerse ourselves in a situation that is different than the last one we were in, we are in transition. The highest of performers understand that in order to bring optimal energy to any task at hand or any situation they're in, they must master these transitions by reflecting on what energy they want to bring and what energy they want to receive.

I learned this from Brendon Burchard's *High Performance Habits*, and it has truly changed my life. While in transition mode, and this could be the largest of transitions like moving countries, or the smallest like getting out of bed to take a shower, stay still for a moment and repeat in your head, "Release." Release all the tension in your body that you are feeling. Your neck, shoulders, legs, arms—all of it. This will get your body in optimal position to receive the cues from your soul as to what energy you want to give and receive in this situation.

After you have "released tension," go ahead and "set intention." This is where you ask yourself, "What is the energy I want to bring to this? How do I want to radiate the zest that is in me for this particular situation and for what purpose?" Then ask yourself what energy you want to receive from this situation. By determining this ahead of time, you are not only setting a cue in your brain to receive only that energy, but you are also setting a cue in your brain *not* to receive any other type of energy.

Have you ever been in a meeting or presentation that maybe didn't go so hot, but the presenter was fired up afterward, and all you could think was *Why? That was an absolute train wreck; why are they so excited?* It was probably because they were very intentional with the energy they wanted to receive. They only wanted to receive the positive energy, so their brain was not only cued to receive the positive but not receive the negative.

I recently gave a presentation for my physical and financial wellness business. I partnered with a cute girl to do the presentation. I could tell she was a little nervous, but I was fired up and ready for it. Beforehand I got very clear with my "release tension, set intention" practice and decided the only energy I wanted to give off was that of optimism, motivation, and excitement. The energy I wanted to receive was support, positivity, thrill, and engagement.

After the presentation it was fascinating to hear how my presenting partner thought the presentation went. She thought it went horribly. She said no one was engaged or interested, and the energy was "low." On the other hand, I had a completely different experience. When I was speaking every woman in the room was off her phone with her eyes on mine, engaged, focused, and asking questions. I thought the vibrancy was popping and the engagement was at an optimal level.

It goes to show that if you get clear with the energy you want to attract from the start, that is the energy you will receive. I was fired up after that meeting, ready to take more action in my business, talk to more people, and further my confidence in building this business; my presentation partner took a few days off because she felt discouraged. I made great headway and had one of my biggest weeks ever in my business to that time, while my presentation partner regressed.

Whatever energy you are committed to sending out and receiving in the world is the energy you are going to get. It can either fill you up or tear you apart. Before any transitional moment in your day, stop. Take a second. Breathe. Repeat the word *release* over and over again until all the tension is released in your body, and you feel like a cooked spaghetti noodle.

Then set your energy intentions. Really dig deep, and reflect on the environment or experience you're about to be immersed in and how you can add value to it through your energy. What type of energy does this environment need for you to make it the best it can be and also help you advance in becoming the best *you* you can be? Ask yourself what kind of energy you want to receive. I'm sure you've heard the term *energy vampire* before, and yup, they are out there. They will suck the life right out of you if you're not careful. However, if you radiate positive, uplifting, motivating energy, that is the energy you will receive from the universe. In fact you can condition your brain to refuse to accept any type of energy that tears away from your heart of service and your mission to love.

Be your own zest. Go zest up your life like that lemon wedge! It's time to radiate love, light, and energy from your heart. In doing that, you'll attract others who do the same.

TAKE NOTE:

1. Every day set intention for the energy you want to give and receive. The reality is that you attract what you project, so if you project negative, doubtful energy, it is those kinds of people that you will attract into your life in return. Every morning spend a few minutes visualizing and contemplating how the best version of you will show up that day. What will you say in the face of an obstacle? How will you act toward others? What energy will you project?

2. Set intention by writing down, on a piece of paper or in your journal, your daily 3WP. Your 3WP is your *three-word protocol*, and it defines the three characteristics you truly want to embody that day. Every day after I write down my 3WP, I also put it in the reminders on my phone. I have the reminders set at 8:30 a.m., 1:00 p.m., and 7:00 p.m. When these reminders go off, they read the three words I chose for that day. Today my three words were patience, kindness, and an abundant source of light (yes, they can be phrases). Each time the reminder goes off, it cues me to consider whether my energy is embodying those values that I set for myself that morning.

3. When faced with a transitional moment (big or small), and you feel the tension rise in you, remember Brendon Burchard's "release tension, set intention" technique. Repeat the word *release* in your mind until you can feel the tension slowly lift. Then close your eyes and *set intention* for the moment you are about to undergo. Who are you going to show up as in that moment? Who will the best version of you show up as?

4. Your perception all is made within the mind. Your intention stimulates your mind to perceive things in a certain way. Setting intention allows you to attract and notice only the energy you intentionally choose to pick up on. By predetermining your intention for your energy, your entire perception and takeaways of the situation will shift toward how you decide to see it. If you intend to have abundant, engaging energy, after giving a presentation you will see the audience more than likely as having been an abundant source of engaging energy as well.

CHAPTER 8

Be Your Own Heartbreak

We've all been there—*breakups*. They suck. They hurt. They feel like a giant black hole of darkness that is sucking all the life out of you.

I remember my first breakup. I was in high school. It all started in Mrs. Emerson's eighth-grade English class. I had the biggest, most enormous, fattest crush on this guy and it was the first time shy Annie had ever actually had a try at being flirtatious. Let's just say I majorly sucked at it. He ended up liking one of my best friends instead. It kept on that way until ninth grade, when we found each other again in Mr. Peebles's religion class.

Important thing to note: the summer before ninth grade I had matured a little bit in the looks department. So the flirtation sprouted back up in that religion class, and you can guess the rest of the story. Girl falls for boy, boy falls for girl; everything is rainbows and sunshine and about anything you can expect from a high school relationship where all you had to worry about was connection, love, and lust, not having the pressures of kids, taxes, jobs, in-laws, or money.

He was my first everything, and I mean *everything*. This isn't easy for the Christian in me to admit, but he was. My first time holding hands, my first dance, my first kiss, the first guy to bring me a gift, my first sleepover with a guy, and yes, the first guy I gave myself to. I guarantee you my father just reread that sentence to make sure he read it right and might be having a heart attack right now. But it's true. All of it.

I gave this guy everything I had to give, the most valuable of that being my heart. If this guy had told me to move to Chicago with him, I probably would have. If he said he wanted to drop out of school and move to California and start up a taco truck for a living, I would have gone with him (in fact I remember us jokingly talking about that). I was fourteen years old when we started dating and sixteen when we broke up. My brain wasn't even fully developed, so why the hell did I think my heart could be? Yet in those moments with him, I felt it. I felt that radiant love that I thought at the time would last forever. Looking at him, I saw forever. It never crossed my mind that there would come a day when I would not have him, but that day came. I still remember that the night before he broke my heart into about a million pieces, he texted me that classic pre-breakup text, "Can we talk tomorrow?" I mean, hello! Of course I knew what that meant! We'd been dating for almost a year and a half, so since when do you have to ask to talk to me?

That night I knew that he was about to break my heart the next day, which may I remind you was two days after my car accident on Atlanta Highway 285. Lest I say he couldn't control this, the timing was just horrible. Thing was, I was ready for it in a way. I can't explain it, but something in me felt as though this was the next step God intended for me to take. It was time to grow in ways that I couldn't with my boyfriend at that time.

Just like that, he broke up with me the next day. Yes, it hurt; yes, I tried to find the good in it and remember that feeling of readiness I felt the night before. But no, that temporary feeling of readiness for the breakup didn't last long, and after the dumping I was completely shattered. It felt as if my heart had been ripped out of my body and stomped on. I had no appetite, no desire for tennis, and seeing him felt like a bullet through my heart. Going to a high school with about five hundred students while trying to avoid someone, definitely adds a whole new layer of difficulty to your motives, not to mention the struggle of having sixth-period history together.

You know how in movies, a while after the breakup, both people seem to move on, and each is actually happier without the other person? Yeah, that didn't happen for me. In fact it wasn't until I got out of that damn school, graduated, and went to college that I finally let go of my high school boyfriend. Yes, it took that long (we broke up at the beginning of junior year).

During those last years of high school I completely dedicated myself to tennis, focusing on getting a scholarship at a school I absolutely loved so I could fulfill my dreams of playing college tennis. All this was good, but my motives behind focusing on tennis were not beneficial to my emotional and mental well-being. You see, I was using tennis as my coping drug of choice. The more I focused on tennis and things related to tennis, the less I felt as if I would allow myself to think about my ex-boyfriend.

It was a nice Band-Aid at times, but that pain of feeling not good enough and having my heart shattered never got the chance to heal because I never confronted it. I just let it sit there, burying it repeatedly the best I could. I wouldn't let myself think about him or how he'd hurt me. This only caused me to think of him more and more and come up with hopeful possible explanations in my head of how he might still possibly love me or how the reason he broke up with me was that "you always let go the things you love." In fact, Passenger's song "Let Her Go" came out right about this time, which only added fuel to my false hopes.

In a word, I was guarded. I never wanted to feel that pain again—ever. I wanted to wall myself up the best I could, tuck away my heart, and hide it from any boy in sight. I swore off boyfriends and dates; even the thought of marriage I erased from my mind. The only thing love reminded me of was pain, torture, and something that never lasts forever. I had the brain tattoos that "all men will break your heart" and "no relationship can ever possibly last forever."

Then I met the next guy I would give my heart to. This guy is still to this day in my opinion one of the most phenomenal people, and I wish him all the best. I believe God puts people into your life for instrumental purposes: to grow you in ways you cannot grow yourself. This guy was one of those instrumental figures for me. Thing is, I also believe God pulls those people out of your life once they have done their job of getting you to where you need to be and are no longer a benefit to your life, and that He did as well with this person.

Before I go on, no, this relationship was not "the one" and did not last. Yet it taught me probably the most important thing about love that I have learned thus far as a twenty-year-old, that love comes in all shapes and forms and with all types of people; sometimes it lasts forever, and sometimes it isn't meant to. But that doesn't mean the relationships that don't last forever mean nothing.

The bravest thing you can do in this world is to love. After my first boyfriend I thought I was being all tough and mighty by living out my independence: I'm a strong, independent young woman who don't need no man! I thought I was the bravest that you could get, not relying on any boy to fix my problems.

Falling for my next boyfriend revealed to me the greatest secret of all time: being brave means not hiding yourself from the world and what it has to offer. Brave is not guarding your heart with walls so high that no one can get in, even if you truly believe you can do everything on your own.

Brave is realizing that relationships aren't there to fix you or change you. Relationships with the right people are meant to take you farther than you could ever take yourself. A healthy relationship is not the means to for two people to fill up one another's holes but a linking-up of two whole people contributing to each other in ways that give them a greater impact than they would have alone. They are meant to add value to your life and make your light shine brighter than it ever could on its own.

Heartbreak sucks, yes, it does. It hurts and wounds and feels at times as though someone is actually sucking all the oxygen out of your lungs as slowly as possible. When my first college relationship ended, for the first four weeks I couldn't make it through one class without having to excuse myself to the bathroom, start sobbing, and immediately call my mom or sister or dad or anyone who'd pick up the phone to tell me it would all be all right.

You know how they say love is blind? Yeah, I believe that in a lot of ways. When you're in love, you're blind to anything you don't want to see; it's almost as if you're looking through a microscope, and whatever that microscope isn't focused on will not be in your view. When I thought my college boyfriend and I would be together for a long time, I believed that absolutely; I was blind to all the big red flags that said, "Annie, no! This isn't it! It is something great, yes, but there's something more."

God will truly keep breaking your heart until it opens. We are born as free, wide-open, careless, loving creatures with no walls or guards around our hearts. We have not experienced anything yet to make us feel the painful side of love; all we know to do is receive care from our caregivers (food, water, affection) who provide us with unconditional love, and that's our awareness of love as far as we know it: it's unconditional. As we get older, we experience more. Everyone experiences some form of heartbreak, and some experience things like abuse or neglect, making their walls grow up around their hearts more and more. It's not intentional, but it's simply the body's way of protecting itself from the pain that can come from love. That's why after my high school boyfriend broke my heart, I guarded it with the freaking Great Wall of China, until college.

Something shifted in me after my college relationship ended. I decided to handle things differently. I didn't want to be guarded again. I didn't want to wall up and never trust another boy again. Yes, it sucked to have my heart broken another time, but looking back at both relationships, I also realized all the ways I had grown as a woman that I wouldn't have if I'd never had the guts to get into those relationships and fall in love.

Instead of hiding myself away from boys of all sorts and never truly opening my heart up to people, I decided to go a completely different route and open myself up completely. Whatever relationship in whatever form came my way, I wanted to make sure I was the biggest-hearted and most loving person I could be in every relationship I had. I wanted to make not just another person I got into a relationship with feel loved but anyone and everyone I interacted with feel so incredibly loved by me that they could feel it in their hearts.

I can honestly say that while I think the absolute world of the first boy that I dated in college, it took me just a few months to truly heal from that heartbreak—as opposed to the years it took in high school, when I decided to wall myself up and guard my heart after my heartbreak. Now you could say I had much deeper feelings for my first boyfriend, and that's why it took longer to get over him, but that wouldn't be true.

I firmly believe that the most powerful source of healing is love. Hatred, guardedness, caution, pain—they only stir the pot of tension in your heart from whatever heartbreak you went through. Holding something against someone and guarding your heart from experiencing new loving relationships, because of one person who broke your heart, only gives that person incredible power of you. Over time it will stop affecting them, but it will continue to infect you with the toxicity of those negative emotions. Don't let them have that power. If you choose to open your heart and embrace the growth you experienced and the incredible person you became through the pain and the progress, that is where your greatest healing lies.

There is no such thing as a failed relationship. Even the most toxic relationship is not a waste of time, and we shouldn't look at it as something to regret. It is our interactions with others, especially significant others with whom we are most intimate, that teach us the most about ourselves, our values, and what matters to us when we are at our worst and at our best.

Don't hide yourself from the opportunity to grow and see just how much love God has blessed you with. Yes, it's true that you may get your heart broken. However, as one of my favorite country bands, Florida Georgia Line, says, "If it's meant to be, it'll be," because if not, God has something so much better for you in store.

Have the courage to keep putting yourself out there. Get yourself into situations where your heart could be broken; it is there that you will find undeniable strength, growth, and more *love* than you ever thought possible.

TAKE NOTE:

1. When you experience heartbreak, be conscious of your coping strategy of choice. Are you pursuing other things as a distraction from dealing with the hurt or a means to generate happiness in your life amid the heartbreak? It is *good* to find hobbies, friends, things to cope with! However, do not let that stop you from facing the pain you are feeling and letting it make you stronger. Journaling changed my life when I realized that writing things out helps me unleash buried anxieties, fears, and worries, some of which I didn't even know were there. The greatest icons of all time keep a journal. Start trying to journal for at least five minutes a day, and then bump it up. It is a wonderful tool to get your deepest worries out without fear of judgment.
2. Remember that heartbreak is natural, normal, and commendable. You are not weak for feeling brokenhearted. That brokenness is a symbol showing you just how vulnerable you allowed yourself to be, and the bravest thing to do in this world is to make your heart vulnerable. After some time has passed, think of the ways you became stronger throughout that relationship. Also, integrate into your identity that you went through a massive heartbreak

and survived. Nothing is stronger or more beautiful than a broken heart that continues to live and love. You are a badass if you have gotten your heart broken and still get up every day to love your siblings, your parents, your friends, your neighbors .... In fact, continuing to love anyone after getting your heart broken demonstrates incredible strength.

3. There is no such thing as a failed relationship. Ask yourself, "What else could this mean?" What could God, the universe, or whatever you believe in be trying to show you? I guarantee you, if one door has closed, there is an open window that you haven't ever seen. Look for the window of opportunity. Ask yourself, "What could God be trying to show to me here?"

CHAPTER 9

Be Your Own Beautiful

Growing up, I never really considered myself "beautiful." I never thought I was ugly or anything, but I never felt as if I was drop-dead gorgeous either. My high school seemed to breed only supermodels—you know, the kind of girls whose bodies are stick figures, yet they still somehow have boobs and their hair is always flawless. Yeah, those were the girls in my high school. My spirally, crazy curls didn't feel right among their pin-straight glossy hair, and I never felt like I was pretty until my freshman year of high school.

Let me tell you, the reason my sudden confidence in the looks department decided to sprout up wasn't because I grew big boobs and a big butt or was blessed overnight with natural olive skin and Selena Gomez's hair during a Pantene commercial. It was all tied to right about the time I got that first boyfriend of mine. When I found out the first guy I ever dated liked me back, that was the first time I'd ever really considered myself attractive or somewhat good-looking. My reasoning was *If my boyfriend is attracted to me, then that must mean I've got to be somewhat pretty, right? I mean, what guy in high school would want to date someone who wasn't pretty?*

Now there's a lot wrong with that mind-set, and the fact I completely put my perception of my beauty in the hands of whether or not a boy found me attractive is just scratching the surface, but at the time that's the perspective I had: If a boy likes you, you are pretty. You are good enough. You are attractive. However as time went on, I kept finding myself trying to fit into the ideal "girlfriend material" stereotype. This meant trying to have the perfect hair, the perfect body, and the perfect personality.

Before I go any further, I want to say that, no, this was by no means my ex-boyfriend's fault; this was all me. In my head I thought I had to be a certain way and have a certain look to gain his affection and love; I molded myself into what I thought was acceptable and good enough for him. I went on crazy diets—you know, the ones where you plan to cut out bread for a whole year but then two weeks later cave and go to LongHorn to have a whole loaf of their delicious brown bread to yourself before your actual dinner even comes. Yup. I did them all.

What this led to was a huge insecurity in my body and eventually an eating disorder. I'd go to tennis practice for sometimes up to five hours a day and come home to feed myself only carrots or celery. At first I was really pleased; it worked. Even my boyfriend at the time said I looked good, and my friends were saying how lean I looked. My shorts were starting to look better on me, those Lulu tennis tank tops I'd always shoved to the bottom of my dresser because they were too tight actually suited my body now, and in photos I liked the way I didn't have to spend a million hours trying to find the right angle where my back fat didn't fall out of my sports bra.

After my boyfriend and I broke up, it got worse. Eventually the pains in my stomach from not eating got so bad that this habit of non-nutritious eating (also known as celery and rice cakes) slowly turned into a never-ending cycle of depriving myself one day and then binge-eating the next day. I would do my normal routine one day, go to practice, and come home to eat nothing but veggies or fruit, but the next day because the pains in my stomach were so bad, I'd eat everything in sight. Any food in the kitchen, I'd eat it. I couldn't control myself. In my head I justified it with "Well, I didn't eat anything yesterday, so I can eat anything I want right now." It was almost like I was on autopilot going through the motions, unaware of how much I was eating. I would go to bed that night with my stomach still in pain but a different kind of pain. I had eaten so incredibly much that it actually felt as if my stomach would burst.

One night in particular, after I had binged, my mama came into my room to ask me what was wrong. She knew something was up because I was going to bed at around 7:00 p.m. I tended to go to bed super early a lot in high school, and even though I did get up early, it was also a way to ensure I wouldn't be tempted to eat anything else that night.

On this night, when Mama came in, I was in fetal position because my stomach hurt so badly from eating so much that I couldn't sleep any other way. I was crying my eyes out when she asked me if I was okay. I can fake a smile to a lot of people, but my mom and dad are two people who never buy my fake happiness, no matter how hard I try. "I hate my body. I hate myself. I hate how I look. I hate who I am. Why can't I be pretty and skinny like the other girls?"

Every morning I would look at my tummy in the mirror. Whether it looked flatter or tubbier than the previous day would make or break my day right then and there. I would either be on cloud 9 (that my stomach looked flat), which led me to have a happy, beautiful view on life that day, or I'd be devastated because I thought I looked bigger, leading into a day filled with self-loathing and hatred.

This progressed for the rest of my high school years until, right before college, I really decided to get my act together nutritionally. I wasn't going to let my insecurities in high school follow me to college. I dedicated myself to an amazing nutritional program that has completely changed my life and finally shown me what the meaning of true beauty is. I did not go through therapy, yet because food issues are widespread and a very serious problem for many, especially in the United States, I highly encourage anyone who is experiencing one to seek out help.

What I have realized over the years is that eating disorders of all kinds—binge eating, bulimia, anorexia, or any of the others I did not list—do in fact have a common foundation, even though the means to that disorder vary so widely. That foundation is a lack of self-love and appreciation. If we do not appreciate ourselves, love ourselves, and want what's best for ourselves, then we will abuse ourselves. If you truly love yourself, you will want to fuel your body with the right nutrition. You will want to give it the food that it needs to be healthy and vibrant. You will want to have a healthy relationship with food, exercise, your mind, and your body because you understand that in order to be your best you, the you that you love, you need to have a strong relationship between those factors.

My mother always says that the wellness company my business is partnered with is a "self-development company with a compensation plan and wellness products." I couldn't agree more. Doing the inner work, revealing aches in my heart that I hadn't touched on since I was a little girl, working through the pain of my self-loathing and hatred—all that finally gave me solid confidence and an unshakable love for myself and thus my body. When I could love myself for everything that I was and was not, I wanted my body to be fueled with the best nutrition out there because I wanted it to be its best self every single day.

Beauty is not what you see in magazines. It is not the Photoshopped perfectly thin girl on the billboard who has a tiny waist, huge butt, big boobs, flawless olive skin, and hair that glistens in the sunshine. It is not the number you see on the scale. It is not the perfectly toned arms of the famous Instagram personal trainer you stalk daily. It isn't the color of one's skin, the shade of one's eyes, the tint of one's hair, or their type of mascara. I know I may sound like your high school guidance counselor, but please hear me when I say, *Beauty is not an outward appearance; it is an energy.*

The most beautiful people on this planet are those who have the incredible energy of self-love, devotion, and passion—those so overflowing with love for themselves that they have enough love to pour onto other people. Beautiful people are people who care, people who listen, people who are interested in what others have to say and are curious about what is going on around them.

Beautiful people are passionate. Have you ever talked to someone who's completely geeking out about a certain passion of theirs, whether it's reading, writing, skydiving, or military history? It is absolutely beautiful to see someone talk about something they love to do and can lose themselves in. Beauty is the energy you receive from someone who talks about something they are passionate about.

Beauty is also someone's ability to be completely and utterly them. There are countless ads, TV shows, billboards, and posters telling people how they should look and where they should go to look a certain way. Beauty is not found in morphing yourself into someone else's standards of what they think beauty is. Beauty is accepting who you are physically and exploding with who you are mentally, emotionally, and spiritually from the inside out. It is knowing who your soul is and being connected with your inner sense of path and purpose, leaving only space for you to be completely and entirely you. People who dance to the beat of their own drum, that is beautiful.

Too many times we think we're not good enough, skinny enough, fit enough, or short enough, and too many times we keep striving for this sense of "pretty" and "beautiful" instead of enjoying where we're at with the body we're at. Why is it that most girls who experience eating disorders simultaneously experience depression? And why is it that even when women reported to have obtained their ideal weight are still depressed? It is because no matter how much you try and try to be society's definition of "beautiful" on the outside, beauty is not an external achievement. Beauty is an energy from the inside.

Do I believe in becoming your healthiest self so you can exude the energy needed to be your best self? Absolutely. But I do not promote trying to become skinnier or curvier or fitter if it means sacrificing your own health to do so. Beauty cannot be obtained externally. You must dig deep and do the interior work in order to find that beautiful energy inside you to exude each and every day.

This energy can't be ordered on Amazon, found in Target, discovered in a Weight Watchers brochure, or revealed on an episode of *Dr. Phil*. Sorry to break it to you, but you cannot buy beauty despite all the ads and fads to the contrary. The key to beauty is the energy inside you that is uniquely and purposefully created to be held only by you, the energy that lights up your heart, mind, body, and soul. You have this in you right now. You don't have to go on a European extravaganza to "find yourself," buy that new diet program, or get the newest clothes off that Instagram clothing store that pictures that hottest trends on the hottest people. You are beautiful right now, just by expressing the energy inside you. When people feel their most disconnected and depressed, they simultaneously feel their most insecure about their outward appearance. This is because they are not connected with the beautiful, divine energy inside them. They are not connected with their beauty.

Your ears, your eyes, your hair, your face, your skin, your legs, and your thighs rubbing together were all given to you as means to express your beauty, not means to define your beauty. Your body is simply the vehicle you were given to transport your energy to the world. That energy, the one given to you to share with the world because the world is craving for it, that is your beauty. Be your own beautiful. Let your body do its part by acting as the vehicle for your energy to be projected to this world, the energy that lights your soul on fire.

TAKE NOTE:

1. I am not sure what you are going through when it comes to your appearance. You may be dealing with an eating disorder such as I had like bulimia or binge eating, body dysmorphia, or maybe you don't have a "disorder" but have just been a jerk to your body recently for not being big enough, strong enough, skinny enough, or whatever. Try this exercise. Each morning I used to look at my stomach, and whether it was flat or not would lay the groundwork for my self-perception that day. When I was recovering from this disorder, I had the idea of never allowing myself to look at my tummy but instead to gaze at my smile. I shifted my focus from my stomach to my smile and stared at that every single morning. I let my smile lay the groundwork for my self-perception that day. It led me to understand that my smile is the most beautiful part of me and the part that matters most. Try this with either your smile or your eyes. That is your never changing beauty. That is where who you are as a person shines through.

2. Remember, beauty is an energy, not a physical appearance. How is it that we see couples where one of them looks like a supermodel and the other may not be the most physically attractive person? Energy. I guarantee you that person has incredibly beautiful energy. The good thing about this? We can only change our physical appearance to a certain extent, but your energy? That is yours for the shaping. Shape it to be your idea of beautiful.

3. Every morning jot down your "10 I Am." These are ten things you find beautiful about yourself. Write these ten things down with confidence, grace, and passion. Don't be afraid of being cocky or egotistical! No one is going to see this; besides, if you cannot name ten things you love about yourself, then this is the exact exercise you need to be practicing every single morning. I could absolutely write down at least ten things (probably even fifty) I

love about myself right off the bat if you asked me to right now, simply because I have practiced it. I have gotten to know myself so well that I am able to praise what I love about myself and also identify what I need to work on. Practice loving yourself! You are beautiful! Do your "10 I Am" every morning.

CHAPTER 10

Be Your Own Opportunity

I used to think positive people were people that never got upset. Positive, happy people were these rainbow-pooping, glitter-sneezing unicorn-esque people who never experienced pain or got upset or were ever hurt. They always were smiling, giggling, jumping and down with joy, making others smile and laugh, and just loving on life and people. Before I got into my first relationship, I thought I was one of those kinds of people. I was always happy, always smiling, always perky and bubbly, simply because there was nothing in my life at the time not to be happy about.

In fact, my life was pretty darn great. I was starting to talk to my first potential boyfriend, tennis was awesome, I had the most amazing friends and wasn't worrying about taxes or money or mortgage, and my whole family was healthy, alive, and were my best friends. After my first boyfriend and I broke up, I remember thinking that I had lost *her*—that girl who was always happy, never felt pain, was never sad, and never cried. I had lost the girl whose cheek muscles were sore at the end of each day from the nonstop genuine smile on her face. I blamed my ex for bringing sadness, grief, and anxiety into my life because that made me lose my "happy Annie."

What I failed to realize as a young girl is that the positivity, happiness, and pure joy that radiates from people is not something they are just born with or a gift that they genetically possess. It does not get "lost" in the changing seasons of life either. In our lives we all have seasons of sadness, anxiety, nervousness, joy, happiness, and bliss; throughout each season the most powerfully optimistic people on this planet choose to be radiant, happy, and positive. They do not let a circumstance come in and take away that part of them.

They define their circumstances, even the most challenging of them, as means for growth and stepping-stones along their path of success. A bend in the road is only the end if you do not make the turn. This is how the icons of our time view their pathway to mastery: no bend is the end because when a bend or a challenge occurs, they simply change direction.

Take the obstacle as feedback that it is time to pivot and try something else. It does not redefine you negatively or make you a failure unless you let it. If anything, it strengthens the person who you have always been. If you have always been grateful, appreciated, loving, and kind, if you embrace the challenges in life as growing opportunities, they only highlight those characteristics in you even more. The contrary is true as well: if you are someone who falls into self-pity, self-loathing, hatred, and fear, obstacles will bring that out if you let them.

This was shocking news to me once I reached college. It wasn't until then, when my patience, happiness, and positivity were once again tested with a different relationship—my relationship with tennis—that I learned this lesson. After my high school boyfriend and I broke up, that "happy girl" started to come back, yes, but for all the wrong reasons. Yes, I was smiling more, laughing more, and giggling more, like my old self, but I still wrapped my mood and happiness up in the circumstances I was in. I never really dug in and dealt with the pain I felt from the breakup in high school; it was too painful.

So what did I do? I shoved that sucker down. I was not about to confront it or deal with it, because if I had to do that, then I would have to admit it was there in the first place. I would have to admit to myself just how much I loved him and how much it hurt when he broke my heart. I was not about to put myself through that pain. No, thanks! I was just going to shove it down because all I wanted was to be "that girl" again—the happy girl with no problems and no worries. I was so set on getting back to her that I wasn't ready to accept that I'd actually gone through something painful and that I needed to do the work to get through it and then get back to *her*, but happier than before.

Nope, I just wanted to flip a switch: one day heartbroken, the next day all good. So I dove into tennis and getting a chance to play in college.

I made this my life. I was always playing tennis. Completely by choice too; no pressure from my parents or my friends or my coaches or anyone. I couldn't count the times I heard "Annie, I just worry you're not having enough fun" or "Annie, just take some time off and relax." Thing is, the more I poured myself into tennis and devoted my energy into this goal of playing college tennis, the less I thought about the pain from that breakup. The pain was still very much there, but tennis was a nice Band-Aid to the hurt for the moment. However, I soon found that, as my girl Taylor Swift would say, "Band-Aids don't fix bullet holes." All that pain I was shoving down wasn't going to go away without a fight.

Yes I got a spot on the team and got a chance to play D1 tennis, but I wasn't in the lineup my freshman year. All that hard work felt useless and pointless, and all of a sudden I didn't have that Band-Aid of tennis. For the first time all that pain and insecurity from years past that I hadn't dealt with came up again. That's the funny thing about pain: no matter how much you try to shove it down, fold it up, throw it away, hide it, or even disguise it, it comes back, sometimes more painful than before. I felt \insecure, unsure, and vulnerable. I had no mask, no cover-up, nothing to disguise all my insecurities for the first time since my heart had been broken years past.

Not being in the lineup was way more than simply not playing in a tennis match to me. It was a time when I felt raw and naked. It was an experience that stripped away all the armor I had put on to keep the world from seeing all the pain and heartbreak I had built up but never let myself feel—all because I wanted to go back to being that "happy girl" way too soon.

Here's the thing about heartbreak, bad experiences, and moments of complete and utter destruction that I truly did not understand or want to understand at the time: There is an opportunity. There is something you can grow from if you look for it. Nothing happens to you just for kicks and giggles in this universe. Every huge heartbreak in your life is molding you into the person you were destined to be. If you do not let yourself feel the pain from those heartbreaks, you aren't being strong or tough; instead, you are blocking yourself from growing into the person the universe is trying to shape you into.

Every single time I am going through something that tests my patience, happiness, or energy, I ask myself the question WTOH? "What's the opportunity here?" I got this from the amazing Robin Sharma in one of his mastery sessions, and let me tell you it was absolutely life-changing. (Quick digression: For those unaware of Robin Sharma, he is a world-renowned personal mastery mentor and speaker. You can find him online at personalmastery.com, or check one of his books, including *The Monk Who Sold His Ferrari*. To respond to the thought I know is already crossing your mind, no, I wasn't paid to write that, but yes, you definitely should go check him out.) If you can train your mind-set to a solution-based programming instead of a complaining-based programming, your life will completely change. It doesn't matter if someone just broke your heart into a million pieces, or someone simply cut you off in traffic on the way to Walmart; whatever the situation may be that tests your character, your values, or your attitude, *use* it to find an opportunity for growth.

Do this by first assessing the situation for what it truly is; I don't mean what you personally think it is, but the reality of the situation. More often than not, we deem our circumstances to be much worse than they actually are. When I was benched from the lineup my freshman year, I felt as if somehow everyone in the school knew I wasn't playing and that everyone saw me as nonathletic. Worse, I myself believed that I was a wimpy athlete, that I was horrible at tennis, and that no one would take me seriously as someone who considered herself a D1 tennis player; heck, I even thought I was a joke. I didn't even feel worthy enough to wear clothing that said *Wofford Women's Tennis* because I felt like a fraud.

Let me be clear: I was doing all the workouts, weights, and conditioning each and every day; I simply wasn't playing in the lineup. I damn straight was an athlete and a hell of a good one at that! Still, my perspective on the situation blew up so much that these lies I told myself made it seem much more unbearable that it actually was. There were plenty of athletes at Wofford that didn't play in the lineup, especially since in tennis you can only field six players per match; way more than six were on my team!

I did not assess the situation for what it actually was; instead, I took all my internal chatter as reality. What I needed to do and what you need to do with whatever obstacle you are facing in life is ask yourself, "What is *actually* happening here?" Not what your mind is saying is happening, but what is the reality? I bet you it is not nearly as blown-up catastrophic as you may think. In fact, I'm sure that all those people at the office you think are talking behind your back about the promotion you didn't get but were expecting to, aren't. I guarantee that the lady at the supermarket who gave you a weird look because you were using a ton of coupons, and you think now she must know about your financial struggles, probably just got a bad whiff of something and had to make a face.

My point? You create in your mind what you think of situations. Happiness and suffering are both created in the mind. Which means the paths to both happiness and suffering start there too. You can choose either one based on how you see the situation. That all starts with seeing the situation for what it actually is, not what your ego blows it up to be. You can do this by getting input from a third party (a friend, colleague, or spouse, or maybe even your favorite hairstylist), or you can simply make a list. Write down how your ego sizes up the situation, and write down another list with a detached perspective: how do you think a complete stranger would view the situation? Compare the two, and I bet you the reality of the situation lies somewhere in the middle. Once you have a realistic assessment, you can then start on your path to grow from the situation.

Find a reason to turn that situation into a game-changer for your growth that day. You are capable of growing each and every day from little instances that are always testing you. Whether you realize it or not, that phone call where your friend called you out for being an absolute brat at lunch last week? Yeah, that sucks to hear, but what's the opportunity to grow there? Your friend was honest with you; now you know and can learn from it. It can also inspire you to be more honest and open with your friends in return.

You may be thinking, *Okay, Annie, good try, but I'm not a two-year-old in preschool, and little exercises like that only work for little pipsqueaks. I have "big world" problems, and the "WTOH" exercise just isn't going to hold up to the massive problems I'm facing right now.* Listen, I get it. I'm not saying start right off the bat with your biggest problem and go at it with the rainbows-and-butterflies mentality of all right, what are the positives here? My house is about to be foreclosed, but what's the opportunity? My wife of fifteen years just cheated on me, but what's the opportunity? I may lose my job and have four kids to feed, but what's the opportunity?

I understand it when you say that thinking about the opportunistic outcomes from your circumstances sounds worse than sticking pens into your eyes. It can sound a little like a preschool teacher. That's why this is an exercise, though. Like with any exercise, you have got to start small. You're not going to start training for a marathon by running 26.2 miles right off the bat. You'll probably start with two or three miles, then six (a 10K), then maybe ten miles, and build from there. Do the same with this exercise. For the little things that irritate you throughout the day, try to find the opportunity in them. Did one of your classmates bail on your meeting with them to study for your test? Maybe the opportunity is that you can finally be intentional with finding out how you study best independently; you might even focus better without the distraction of another person.

You had the worst day ever at school or at work, and you come home only to have your boyfriend complain about his day? He didn't even ask you once how your day was? The opportunity here could be to work on your listening skills, or if this is something that happens consistently, a courage-strengthening exercise to generate the bravery to address how he never asks about your day, leading to a pivotal point of growth in your relationship.

Bottom line: think deep on how is this going to help your growth? What opportunistic mind-set can you bring to the situation to develop the character, morals, and values of that person you aspire to be? You see, our brain is a muscle. The more we work it over and over again, the stronger it grows. So just as aerobic or anaerobic exercise strengthens the muscles in your body for physical activity, exercises like the "what's the opportunity here?" exercise develop your brain muscles for mental activity. This exercise in particular is working that opportunistic muscle in your brain that seeks out the growth opportunities in difficult situations.

Eventually, with practice, your ability to create opportunity out of a situation that seems to bring nothing but destruction will be almost automatic. Even in the face of large circumstances—being evicted from your home, losing your job, or having your heart broken—you will find yourself asking first thing, "What is the opportunity here?" This will bring you to confront the situation and your pain around it, but not in a way that is enveloped in self-pity. You are facing the pain of the situation with strength in your mentality to find the opportunity amid this circumstance.

You will find a way to grow from it and become even stronger than before because of it.

After my freshman year of college when I was not in the lineup, I realized that no matter what in life, there will always be things that test your happiness and who you are. There will never be a time in your life where everything is perfect so that you can just be happy, giddy, and giggling all the time. Nope, doesn't work like that. Why? Because life is *life*! It has its amazing, incredible, wonderful highs but also its depressing, dark, and heart-scathing lows. It is your choice to either combust along with everything else in your life during the depressing, dark, and heart-scathing parts—*or* you can choose to find the opportunity and grow from it.

If you can develop this "what's the opportunity here?" mentality, you will be indestructible because no matter what is thrown at you, you will see it not as obstacles thrown in your path to push you down but as building blocks for becoming the greater and more amazing you.

TAKE NOTE:

1. You must choose to grow from situations. Growth does not come to those who wish or hope for it but to those who make the decision to actively seek it. Determine the reality of the situation you are in. Make two columns, one of your personal opinions of the situation, and the second of what you may think a stranger's perspective would be on it—or actually ask a friend or significant other or third party about their perspective of the situation. Compare them, and find a happy medium. That is the reality of your situation.

2. To grow from the situation, you must ask yourself *WTOH?* (what's the opportunity here?). Look deep. Take some time to get clear about every single possible aspect of the challenge and every potential thing it could mean. What does this obstacle show me? About myself? My situation? How would my best self respond to this situation as means for growth?

3. Identify three helpful characteristics or values this situation in your life is teaching you that you did not have before or perhaps

had but are now strengthening. Is this challenge developing more courage in you? More patience? More faith or humility?

4. Define three possible outcomes this challenge could be leading you toward that would be helpful to your life. Has there been a dream tugging on your heart the past couple of years, and this obstacle might potentially be a nudge in the right direction?

CHAPTER 11

Be Your Own Anchor

Confession time: When I was younger, I would purposely lose in tennis tournaments just so I didn't have to play another match. (I can feel the grimace my parents just made to themselves.) I used to literally go into the tournament with the mind-set that I just needed to lose two matches and then I'd be done for the weekend (you play at least two matches in all junior tournaments). My wonderful parents were busting their butts taking me to these tournaments, taking time off work and out of their weekends to watch me play, and here I was with the mentality that the sooner I lost, the sooner my weekend could start: I could go get a DQ blizzard (cookie dough for life), put on my dad's big, comfy, overworn sweatshirt, and blare Justin Bieber or the Jonas Brothers on the radio.

Things got tricky when I started to realize that I actually wasn't half bad at this tennis thing. It grew hard to decide whether I should just go ahead and whoop this girl's butt or let her win. *Which one would take less time? If I beat her fast, then the match is over quicker, but if I lose, then I'm done for the weekend.* Oh the struggles of a twelve-year-old tennis player. A part of me cringes to admit this because I am a competitor. I love competing in things that I am passionate about. If I love it and I have a fire in my belly about it, I want to win.

What's also weird is that I didn't want to lose because I hated the sport or hated being there. I wasn't out there intentionally letting the other person win because tennis was this thing that made me so miserable I couldn't stand being on the court one second longer. No, it wasn't even to spite my parents because they sent me out there or anything like that, because they didn't. My wonderful parents couldn't have cared less if I was out there becoming the next Serena Williams or if I told them I wanted to quit; they just wanted me to devote myself to something I was passionate about.

The reason a love-hate relationship with tennis arose for me around that time, enough that I intentionally would lose despite my love for competing, was because of one little thing: *nerves*. It felt as if someone was taking the inside of my stomach and putting it in a blender or a hyperactive washing machine. Every single time before I went on that court, I thought I was about to throw up, and one time I even did. Now granted, this was when I was around ten to twelve years old or so, before I decided that if I was going to be devoting all this time to the sport and gave myself a chance to actually win a match, I could be a really great player with commitment and hard work. Still, I will never forget that horrible nervous feeling.

My body would shake, my palms would break out in profuse sweat, and my attention would be so flighty that if you were talking with me, my eyes would probably be darting all around the room trying to find a way out. If my opponent withdrew (which rarely happened), I'd feel as if I'd won the lottery because for a short period it was relief from the nervousness I would've felt if they hadn't withdrawn and I had to play.

When I got to college, that nervousness didn't go away; in fact, it got even worse. Now I need to point out that I stopped intentionally losing after I entered the fourteen-year-old age group of junior tournaments, but I remember that during my first college match my whole body was overthrown by nerves. My legs were shaking so bad I couldn't even keep my feet on the ground. Every time I hit the ball, my whole body would jump into the air, and the ball would fly out like it wanted to hop out of that match just as much as I did.

I was so scared. What was my new coach thinking? What about my new teammates? Oh my goodness, what about all those cute boys who stopped by to watch? My heart was racing so fast I thought it was going to literally explode. I kept saying to myself, *Stop being so nervous Annie stop being so nervous*, yet that only seemed to make things worse. I couldn't even think about the match I was playing because my mind was consumed by simply how nervous I was. The more I thought about it, the more it freaked me out and the more nervous I became. Here's a twister for ya: I then got nervous about the fact I was nervous. Yes, that is a thing. And no, it does not just happen to me. It brought me back to that memory of why I would lose on purpose: Who would ever want to feel something like this? This sucks. This is not fun. I just wanted to go home.

Fast-forward to my junior year of college. My body still does that thing before tennis matches where my heart starts racing, my palms are sweating buckets, my armpits start getting wetter and wetter until it starts literally dripping down my arm, and my legs start to feel uncontrollably shaky. Something I learned, though, between my freshman year and sophomore year is that you can use nerves to your advantage if you channel them positively.

I realized that, at moments in my life when I was excited and moments when I was nervous, my body had the same physiological reaction. If I get really excited for something, my heart races, my armpits and palms start to sweat, and my legs go numb because I just cannot wait for that moment. So why is it that we can take one reaction from our body and, depending on what connotation we give it (excited or nervous), make it mean a positive or a negative thing? Especially if your body has the same physical response in both scenarios?

The reason your body has the reaction it does is because before any event that is going to bring you out of homeostasis (i.e., your "neutral, day to day, regular state"), it is preparing you for action. It is preparing your body to do something, feel something, or act on something. When your hands start sweating, your eyes starting darting everywhere because your mind is going a million miles an hour, and your legs start shaking underneath you, that is your body's way of warming up for whatever is coming. Let's take a second and wrap our heads around this, shall we? If our body has the same physical reaction for what we perceive to be nervousness and excitement, and how we label that behavior in whatever situation is causing that particular physiological state determines whether we are going into the situation pumped for what's to come, or dreading the experience...why would we NOT label what we're feeling every single time we get that feeling as excited?

Think about how you feel when you think you're excited about something. You're ready for it. You're prepared. You cannot wait for it to happen; in fact, it seems as though it can't come soon enough because you're looking forward to it so much, right? It's a positive experience. Now let's think about how you feel when you're nervous about something. You almost never want the morning of that looming event to come because it's making you so nervous. You want it to go away and never show up in your life again. You want to run away and hide in your room or just want it to stop. It's a negative experience.

What if you tried telling yourself before every situation that gives you that particular physiological response—the sweaty palms, increased heart rate, shaky knees—that you are feeling excitement as opposed to nervousness? Then every single time you get that prepping response from your body's warm-up for taking action, you will consistently go into whatever situation and make it a positive experience from the start as opposed to a negative one. Since nervousness and excitement initiate that same physical response from our body, we can trick our brains into thinking that over time we get that response it is excitement and a positive thing, as opposed to nervousness and a negative thing. This will prevent you from going into a situation with negative expectations and also prevent the "nervousness spiraling" of getting nervous and then getting more nervous about how nervous you are.

Shifting your terminology from *nervous* to *excited* when you describe what you're feeling as your body goes into "prep mode" is one way to ultimately diminish any fear, doubt, or anxiety that creeps up when you're about to do something that pulls you out of homeostasis (your "neutral"). This all ties in again with the concept of self-talk: how you talk to yourself determines the outcomes that follow challenges you face. It helps you anchor down in the situation and present your best self to the situation. By saying you're excited, you'll have an amped, positive attitude going into that situation. Another very important skill to develop when going into situations that test you, challenge you, and even may present surrounding people that will criticize you is the skill of being anchored in your why.

I'm a twenty-year-old college kid. People ask me all the time why I get up every day at 4:15 a.m., why I choose to add to my workload beyond homework and tennis with my business, and why the heck I'd ever voluntarily want to write this very book I'm writing to you right now. No, it's not always easy; no, it doesn't always bring me joy in the moment, and yes, sometimes on a Friday night when my friends are going out to a party but I am staying in because I haven't reached my weekly page quota or done the amount of business work I set for myself to have done, it sucks.

Likewise on Sundays, when my team is driving back from a tournament and goes into a restaurant to order food, yet I have devoted myself to intermittent fasting every Sunday for the major physical and psychological benefits; the looks I get and temptations I feel are not always easy to just ignore. I'm sure you've had similar experiences where you've questioned your purpose for doing something when it seems that what everyone else is doing is the easier way to go or the better thing to be doing. I'm sure some people think I'm a freak, way too type A, too uptight, too disciplined, never having any fun or letting loose, or wasting away the best four years of my life. At times I totally think this too, and that is when the doubt creeps in.

The thing is, my why is way bigger than their criticisms or judgments. My why is way bigger than even my own criticisms, judgments, or fears. If your why is not bigger than the criticism of those around you, then your why is not big enough—or the craft or job you're devoting yourself to isn't a big enough vehicle to fully serve your why.

Whenever the doubt creeps in for me, I think about my why. There are three reasons as to why I do what I do.

1. I want to be the best I can be from the inside out.

The happiest people are also the people who take the greatest care of their body. People simply do not know how amazing their bodies are supposed to feel. When you've gotten to a point in your life where you understand how incredible it is to feel healthy and vibrant, you simply cannot go back. The pain of not feeling amazing surpasses the pain of not being able to eat that donut for breakfast. The pain of your body feeling like crap outweighs the pain of getting up out of bed to go get your exercise in. Eventually, the long-term pain of not feeling incredible in your own body is greater than the short-term joy that donut will give you.

Am I saying I never indulge? Absolutely not! Moderation is key and it is important to balance everything with perspective. But listening to your body should be held to the utmost priority. Your body wants you to be your healthiest self because that will lead your body to show up as its greatest self. Listen to your body, and nourish it properly. Also understand that when your body is hungry, it is craving nutrients, not necessarily calories. It took me forever to learn this, as I always thought, if I was hungry, I could just eat whatever I wanted. But listen to your body to understand that when it is hungry, it needs nutrients, so pick foods that make you feel good. I have a list of foods in my room that I know energize me and help me show up as my best self. Some of these foods include my superfood shakes, avocados, bananas, leafy greens, alkaline coffee, quinoa, and dark chocolate. This way I know exactly what I need to eat to make me feel my best self. Becoming my best self nutritionally leads me to behave my best self morally and leads me to my happiest, most grateful, most vibrant self so I can serve the greatest number of people possible with the twenty-four hours I have within each day. This why pushes me past the judgments and criticism of people when I'm on a cleanse day and they are chowing down on a burger, thinking I am way too stuck up or weird because I do things like intermittent fasting as a twenty-year-old whose metabolism is probably at the peak of its game.

2. I want to make more so I can give more.

I want to be financially free so that I can give to others as much as I wish without having to limit my giving. Many people think money makes you bad, greedy, filthy, or dirty; however, this is not necessarily the case. Having money simply makes you more of the person you already are. If you are a greedy, filthy, snaky person to begin with, then yes, money will only accentuate that in you. However, if you are a giver and a lover, more money will only help you give and love more people than you could otherwise. I do the work of my business so that I can pave my way to financial freedom, so that I can serve and give to others as much as I wish without any restrictions or limits. This pushes me past the fear I have in the back of my mind that I won't be successful at this business, that I'm too young or too inexperienced, and that I am going to fail. It anchors me down for when people attack what I do, say I'm too young, say I work too much, or downplay my successful business to simply a "hobby."

3. I ultimately want to serve as many people as I can nutritionally, spiritually, emotionally, and financially.

I want to pour into others and shine light on THEIR LIGHT, the light inside them. Too many people in this world are blind to the fullness of their own self and the power they have within them. I want to become my best self nutritionally, spiritually, emotionally, and financially so that I can help others become their best self.

As Robin Sharma taught me, your exterior empire only grows as far as you grow your interior empire. Without doing the work on myself to lead a legendary life, how in the world can I expect to influence others to do the work on themselves to lead their own legendary life? Day in and day out, by listening to podcasts or audiobooks, exercising, eating right, working my way toward financial freedom in my physical and financial wellness business, and just simply doing the do, I am expanding my interior empire so I can expand my exterior empire. This exterior empire I'm referring to is the amount of people I can help expand their interior empire. This anchors me down and roots me to my mission. It does not erase any fear, doubt, insecurity, or vulnerability that I feel; I feel all those things every single day. It does, though, expand my confidence, love, and courage to take action so that those things overcome the fear.

Finding your why, or your anchor, is the next thing that will help you break past your fears and discouragement. It will anchor you down so that when you are feeling doubtful or nervous, you can see past those feelings to focus on your mission and your ultimate goal. You could be a taxicab driver; your why might be to brighten the day for whoever gets into your cab because with every single person you can make smile, you are serving humanity. You could be a dentist, and your why is to make sure every single person who comes through your office leaves with impeccably clean teeth so they smile ten times more confidently than they did before coming into your office.

Find your why, and you find your how. Once you know your mission and the reason that is rooted deep in your soul for doing your craft, you will figure out a way to get it done no matter what obstacles are thrown at you in the process. The naysayers, the haters, the financial scares, the nutritional scares—all of it will not be as great as your why. Let this anchor you deep into your mission and serving the world by following your path of purpose.

TAKE NOTE:

1. Everyone gets nervous. Even the most famous, iconic, and legendary figures of all time get nervous. Look at it as your body preparing you to do something big and getting you ready for the next accomplishment you are about to take on.

2. When you catch yourself labeling your feelings as *nervous*, swap out that term for the word *excited*. You're about to give a presentation in front of forty people on your new business idea, and your hands are sweaty and shaky? Awesome, you're *excited*. You're about to go on your first date with that guy who you never thought would say yes to you asking to get a coffee, and you're so nervous he's going to think your laugh is too high-pitched and your armpits are a little moist (yes, I voluntarily wrote the word *moist*), great. That means you are excited. Y'all, I am telling you! Your brain can only tell *excited* apart from *nervous* based on the meaning you give to the words (one is good, and one is bad), since your body has the same physiological response to both. Condition yourself to label your sentiments as excited, and you will put a positive connotation on the situation, which will help you show up as someone proactively seeking the goodness in the situation, not fearing the situation.

3. Define your why. It doesn't have to be three whole concepts, it could be one or two. It could be ten! But write down on a piece of paper (and this may take some brainstorming) what your why is. Take a miniature poster board, or a big piece of duct tape like I did, and put it on your wall or beside a mirror, and look at it every day. Let it be your mantra and what pulls you through the negativity that will come your way if you continue to pursue your goals. If you do not have a why you do not have a how. If you do not have a how, you will never achieve anything that you set out for. You guys, define your why. Go deep in your heart and ask

yourself, Why are you doing all this? What lights you up about what you are trying to accomplish here? Is it the act of serving others? The act of showing up as your best self? Think about it, and write that sucker down.

CHAPTER 12

Be Your Own Standard

My sophomore year of college, I started doing something that not many other kids were doing at the moment: I started growing my own business. I am a professional network marketer for a wellness company that has forever changed my life these past three years. I'm not just talking physically either, even though I look and feel like a completely different person, but I mean mentally, emotionally, and yes, financially. My mama (the one who paved the way in our family by using these products first and then creating financial freedom through its compensation plan) said it best when she said this company is a personal development company with products and a compensation plan attached. I totally agree; in fact I am 100 percent confident I would not be writing this book to you today without having caught the vision of this company and seeking my own freedom through the opportunity it provides.

I was juggling a lot. I had my hardest semester yet at Wofford (biological psychology was the closest thing I've had to a near-death experience). This was on top of being a division 1 collegiate athlete with twenty- to twenty-four-hour weeks of conditioning, weights, practice, running, and match play; training for a marathon, so I had my own mileage to complete each day; and now deciding to jump in full speed on starting my business. "Overwhelmed" does not do justice to the anxiety I felt each and every day. I'd get up at 4:15 a.m. just so I would have time to get my six- to ten-mile run in before the classes, tennis commitments, homework, labs, work, and business calls that filled my day. Sometimes sorority meetings and volunteer opportunities were thrown into the mix as well. I was also dating someone at the time, and finding time to spend together, even though it was a priority of mine, added another layer of stress to what felt like my overflowing plate.

As my semester went on, I began to notice something. I noticed that I started defining myself by my achievements. The standards I started to set for myself were all exterior, circumstantial standards. For example, my standard for the business was to enroll five people a month, have at least three calls a week, and do my reach-outs and follow-ups every single day. My standard for schoolwork was to make all *B*s and *A*s. My standard for tennis was to simply give it my all in everything I did, always have the most energy, and not get injured. My standard for my marathon training was that I would get up and run every single morning without fail, hesitation, or any days missed. Y'all, I mean it when I say that I never missed a day— not a single one of meeting my requirements for that day.

What I started to notice was that if I didn't meet these standards— for example if I got a *C* instead of an *A* or *B*, didn't have good energy at practice, got injured, didn't do my reach-outs or follow ups that day, or didn't have an amazing run, I felt worthless. I felt as if I had done something wrong or was losing "me." Because I had centered my standards around circumstantial, *exterior* principles, meaning things out of my control most of the time, when those things did not turn out as I thought they should, I crumbled.

That's the thing, you guys: you cannot set your standards on something that is controlled or influenced by the environment around you. Now, I know you're probably thinking, *Annie, that's absolute bullcrap; the environment influences everything*, but that's not necessarily true. You *do* have control over the energy and attitude you bring into each situation. Instead of my standard being to make all *A*s and *B*s and then feeling like crap when I got a *C*, I should have framed my standard around trying my absolute best to prepare for the test as best I could. So what if I make a *C*? Did I do everything that I could? Yes? Okay, then I met my standard. So what if I got injured? Did I do everything I could to prevent that injury— eat right, sleep right, and do warmup and recovery right? Yes? Okay, then I met my standard, and the rest is out of my control.

As sophomore year progressed, I not only noticed that the standards I set for myself started to feel more and more out of reach. As school got harder, business got busier, the season took off, and my running increased, I felt like my ability to reach my standards was slipping from my grip. This made me feel like crap—like a big old incapable, worthless, crapcake of failure.

I also noticed that the more I judged myself by my standards (aka my achievements), the more I judged others for their achievements. You guys, this is super hard for me to admit because I've always been someone who has looked at other people as these incredible miracles that walk the earth. But yes, I did, I judged others continuously every day for the standards they held themselves to. Why? Because I was judging *myself* every day by the standards I held myself to. Since my standards were based on external achievement, I held others to the same type of standard—looking at them based on their external achievements. I am not proud of this, and never in a million years would I happily admit this to anyone, let alone write it in a book for the world's viewing pleasure. Thing is, it is so true, and we all do this. We hold others to the standards we hold ourselves to.

If you are a huge workout junky—always in the gym, always eating with your next workout in mind, sleeping with your workouts in mind, and basically just a breathing gym rat who strives to meet the standard of going to the gym six days a week—you are wrapping your identity in that external standard. So if you don't go to the gym six days a week, you either freak out or feel as though you're "losing it"—or both. If that same gym rat were to start dating a girl who rarely ever went to the gym, eventually there would be some tension in that relationship. Why? Because eventually we all hold others to the same standards we hold ourselves to.

This is why it is not just encouraged but absolutely necessary that your standards are not based on external, circumstantial achievements but instead on internal, controllable principles.

For this year of my college career, I set three new standards for myself. I recommend three because that's enough to push you in your accountability but also few enough that your attention isn't scattered on holding yourself to too many principles. My new standards for my junior year of college include consistent gratitude, intentional presence, and no ego.

Each and every day I want to treat as another opportunity to give thanks to my creator for handing me the ability to live, breathe, *smile*, laugh, and love; this is the reason for my consistent gratitude standard.

Another one of my standards is to be absolutely present no matter where I am.

Wherever I am, and whatever task I am doing, I want to give whomever I'm with my full attention and be completely present and in the moment. I was the queen of checklists my sophomore year but struggled a lot with thinking ahead too much. I would have just started one task and would already be thinking about the gazillion other things I had to do that day. Not this year, and never again will I suffer from the anxiety that caused me each and every day. I felt as if I was constantly behind, even though my brain was always one step forward. So to be fully aware, engaged, and present wherever I am with intentional focus is my second standard.

My third standard is *no ego*. This by far is my favorite standard I have set for myself. Our egos hold us back from doing so much. The ego is not just the cocky, greedy, "too cool for school" side of us, even though that's very prominent, but it's also the insecure, vulnerable, and fearful side of us. Let me ask you a question: Whenever you are afraid to do something— post that photo, send that text, ask that person out on a date, or speak up in class or at work—why is that? One might say it's because you're insecure which is true. However, usually it's because you're afraid of what people will think of you. In order to be afraid of what people think of you, you must have it set in your mind in the first place that people are thinking about you—that people care what you do, what you say, what you post, what you send. That my friends, is ego.

I probably just took your mind for a little spin there so go back and reread what I just wrote. My point is that when we are afraid to do something, it is our ego talking. Our ego tells us to sit still, not act, and keep quiet because obviously the whole world is watching our every mood and cares about everything we do and say, so we should just keep a low profile to avoid any judgment, right? Ha! Hate to break it to your ego, but no one really cares all that much. People have way too much going on in their own lives to really give that much attention to what's going on in yours. That's why this is one of my favorite standards I have set for myself: *no ego*. It has allowed me to push past any fear holding me back because of "what others would think" or "how others would react." (More on ego later, though.)

One thing you may have noticed is that all of my standards for myself are controllable. None of them are governed by external situations or circumstances. I have complete authority over my standards, and even if I get a *C*—or heck, even an *F*—get injured, lose a tennis match, bomb my running times, or even sleep through my alarm clock (God forbid), it does not mean that I can't meet my standards that day. I can still be grateful, be present, and have no ego throughout that day, even if *all* of those external circumstances happened. At the end of that horrible day, if it ever happens, I can still say I met my standards and was my best self; instead of ending that day feeling as if I had "lost" myself or was a failure because I did not reach any of my external goals.

This year already I have noticed that because I am holding myself to a different standard, I have started holding people to a different standard. No more is it about whether or not they get up early and go to the gym, their sports record, their grades, or any of their other external achievements; instead, I look at people for their hearts. Do they show kindness? Are they radiating love and gratitude? When I talk to someone, are they engaged in the conversation, asking me questions, looking me in the eyes, or distracted by their phone? Since I hold myself to these standards each and every day, I naturally hold others to them as well.

If you have subconsciously set your standards, or what you hold yourself to every single day, on things that you can rarely control, then you must change them now. Set standards that are internal achievements and can be controlled by you, no matter what happens that day. That is when you'll find that internal bliss in your relationship with yourself and with others, as you hold others to the same standards.

TAKE NOTE:

1. Do not put your worth in things that are fleeting, that is, controlled by something other than yourself. Your worth does not come from anything except what is inside you—things no one else nor the environment can control.
2. A few internal standards that you always have control over:

   - Your attitude
   - Your energy

- Your nutrition
- Your sleep
- Your hygiene
- Your perspective
- Your exercise
- Your self-care regimen
- Your effort
- Your integrity
- Your daily practice of faith
- The people you surround yourself with
- The amount of time you spend on social media and/or watching TV
- The knowledge you choose to receive each day
- How much you are choosing to push yourself out of your comfort zone each day
- Your smile
- The love you give

3. Once you start to hold yourself to standards that you have legitimate control over, you hold others to similar standards. No longer does it matter if they have a 4.0 GPA; do they have a loving heart? No longer is it important that they are MVP of the game; but instead, do they bring a magnetic energy everywhere they go? You judge others to the extent you judge yourself. The standards you hold yourself to are more likely than not the ones that'll carry over onto those you hold the people in your life to.

CHAPTER 13

Be Your Own Release

After the first guy I really fell for decided to end things with me, I struggled a lot with healing the pain. As I said earlier, I didn't confront the pain I felt or the hurt that he had caused me; I just shoved it down hoping eventually it would all disappear. Thing was ... like most things we push out of sight and try to ignore, hoping they'll go away on their own, it didn't go away. In fact, as time went on, the pain just got heavier without me even realizing it.

It wasn't until my next relationship that I realized just how much that heartbreak had taken a toll on me. When my college boyfriend and I first started going out, I refused to say we were dating—not for like the first couple of weeks to keep it casual or anything, but literally for the first three months. We were dating. We absolutely were. We were falling for each other super fast, we acted like we were dating, and we were definitely exclusive. However, the word *dating* or *boyfriend* literally made me want to go running for the hills. This is because I associated the words with pain. In my head, even though I basically had a boyfriend and had all the feelings that a girl would have for her boyfriend, as long as I didn't call him my boyfriend or say we were dating, he couldn't have the power to hurt me the way my high school boyfriend had.

All that pain from my one poor high school relationship experience was coming back up as we continued to get more serious into our first semester of freshman year. I never released the pain I felt when things did not work out with the first guy I truly loved. Instead, I just let it sit there and tried my best to mask it by refusing to date anyone. My intent, it seems, was to convince myself I was better off alone—and relationships never last anyway. At one point I most certainly envisioned myself being single the rest of my life, never getting married, because "love never lasts." Quite the pessimistic attitude, yeah, I know.

Thing was, when I met the first guy I dated in college, I developed very strong but healthy feelings for him. He wasn't about the toxic games that all too commonly take over some relationships, like the old "if you make me jealous, I'll show you I can make you jealous back" game or the manipulation of making me feel bad for something that I should not feel bad about. He pushed me and inspired me, always supporting me in whatever I did. The problem was that, no matter how much I wanted to or how much I tried to, I could not completely open up to him. I could not let him in. It had absolutely *nothing* to do with him! He gave me no reason not to trust him or not to find security in him, but simply because I never did the interior work of releasing my pain from my past relationship, I carried it into my next relationship, which was why that relationship was destined for failure.

I've heard the tale of a professor who brought a water bottle into class, just a plain old water bottle, and held it up in one hand. He asked the class, "How heavy do you think this water bottle is?" The class responded by guessing its weight, but he asked the question again in a different way: "How hard do you think it is for me to carry this right now? How heavy of an effect is it having on the arm that is holding it?"

The class then responded, "Probably not very much. I mean, consider just holding a water bottle with about eight ounces in it; it ain't gonna kill you."

Then he asked another question: "If I continued to hold up this filled water bottle for the next twenty-four hours, how do you think my arm is going to feel?"

The class responded, "It's probably going to hurt really bad."

Now, did the amount of water in the water bottle change at all? No. Did the water bottle itself change at all? No. Did the arm holding the water bottle or the person that arm is attached to change at all? No. So what changed? The amount of time that the arm was holding on to the water bottle. Over time, it got heavier and heavier, even though the initial quantity of water never changed.

This is exactly what happens with obstacles in our life when we do not release them. No matter how big or small, if we let them sit there and do not confront them, even though they don't grow bigger or smaller, they grow heavier. They begin to take more and more of a toll on us because their effect has grown. We may not notice it at first, just like when you first hold a water bottle, you don't struggle to keep holding it up because it isn't that heavy. But over time if you don't confront a situation or obstacle in your life and just let it keep sitting there, it will get heavier and heavier.

I want to dive into this topic a little bit more. These are certain techniques I have used over the past year that have helped me release the tension and negativity troubling me from years past consciously and unconsciously.

1. Meditate.

Meditation has had a controversial reputation in Western culture for many years. At one extreme, people take after the monks and will go to their grave saying it has helped them reach their greatest, most peaceful, and centered state while meditating for hours upon hours. Others will say meditation is what people do who also believe in unicorns, fairy dust, magic potions, and dancing around a fire in the woods to summon the spirits; for them it's a coping mechanism for life's struggles.

I like to consider myself a capable and passionate woman, but I can tell you right now I am not going to spend five or six hours a day meditating. However, I also don't look at meditation as something that will make rainbows appear in the sky and sparkles appear on my skin when I sweat. I digress to say that despite the fact I do not spend five or six hours a day doing it, even though I cannot even imagine the amount of self-awareness and peace that comes with doing so, I am a huge advocate for meditation. I started with five minutes a day. Only five minutes, which *everyone* has. Yes, you who just read that line, you have five minutes too. Someone once said, "He who thinks he doesn't have time to spend ten minutes a day meditating, needs to do it for twenty."

Let me just say, I majorly sucked at it. My mind would dart a thousand directions, and I couldn't think about what my main goal was: to think about *nothing*. I even had angry thoughts directed at my brain because I couldn't get it to stop having thoughts.

I'm going to let you in on a little secret—this is totally normal. It's almost a prerequisite for meditation that at first you have to suck at it. Your brain is like a wild animal; it has thoughts of all types that are days old, months old, and years old. You could be sixty years old still having thoughts that were born when you were twelve. Ordinarily, we never realize this, though, because we are always thinking and going and never give our brains a chance to filter through thoughts that are and are not helpful.

Meditation allows your brain to pause. Once you get really good at it, it acts like a breath of fresh air to a mind that has been cooped inside a box all its life. *Let your mind breathe.* At first you will suck at it. But just as it happened for me, the more you do it, the better you get. It is a skill, and as with any skill, like writing, basketball, teaching, soccer, or public speaking, it requires consistent commitment and devoted time. I am no monk over here—I can honestly say it is a struggle for me to really stay focused on letting my mind breathe for more than seven minutes (I stepped up from five!), but still every day I do it. I like to do it in the morning before my workout. No one is up, and I can think clearly without distraction.

Find a time that works best for you. Start with five minutes and focus on your breath. Then bump it up slowly as you get better and better at it. *Let your mind breathe.* This will give it clarity and make you more centered to let go of the negative conversations your brain is carrying on with itself.

2. Practice Gratitude.

Notice I didn't say express gratitude, think gratitude, be grateful, feel grateful, or what have you. I said *practice* gratitude. Why? Because this too is a skill. It is not easy to be grateful, especially in times of utter frustration and chaos.

However, I have found it to be true, over the past year and a half as I have deliberately practiced gratitude, that gratitude is not in itself an emotion. Because of this it can be felt along with all other emotions. Let me clarify. It is not possible to be insanely angry and intensely happy at the same time. Why? Because they are both emotions. Just like for a majority of the time you cannot be deeply sad while also being immensely joyous, why? Because *they are both emotions.* Since gratitude is a choice, it is not innate or reactive; you can feel gratitude in the midst of anger, happiness, or sadness simultaneously.

When you are grateful during hard situations, you turn those situations into learning experiences and redirect yourself on a path to a more joyous and prosperous outcome. When you practice gratitude, you allow your heart and brain to be filled with such an opportunistic mind-set that you do not have room for negativity (whether doubts from the past, current worries, or anxiety about the future) to seep into your fortified mind. You must *practice* this. In the midst of all emotions and situations find what you can be grateful for. Before bed every night, write down seven things you are grateful for. Why seven? No particular reason. Six is too few, and eight seems a bit too many for most people. *You can find seven things to be grateful for in your day.* I started with seven and am now at fifteen things I write down each night for which I've found gratitude. I can tell when I've had a really crappy day because lines 1 through 5 list my five senses (I can see, I can smell, I can hear, I can touch, I can taste). Sometimes I write down things like the sunshine kissing my skin today. Things like the lady at Walmart holding the door open for me despite her juggling three bags of Kraft Mac & Cheese, cool ranch Doritos, Pampers, and paper towels. Do this every night. Train your brain to find the gratitude. This will help you identify negativity in your thoughts (whether from the past or now), find the thing to be grateful for in them, and shift your perspective. Every day has magic in it if you have the eyes to see it.

3. Journal

One of my favorite authors, Robin Sharma (I've only mentioned him like a dozen times because actually you guys need to get his material), once said, "The softest pencil is always greater than even the sharpest of minds." If you have to go back and read that again to let it sink in, please do. I know it personally took me a second to understand what they heck he was talking about. But you guys, those words are so powerful. I started journaling every single morning for five minutes. I call them my 5p2p (5 pen to paper) minutes. This is where I literally write down anything and everything that is weighing heavy on my heart; if nothing is, I write about my dreams or the things I am grateful for. Really, anything that comes to mind, for five minutes I write about it. I have done this for almost one year now, and it has completely shifted the perspective I carry into each and every day.

Since this is the first thing I do after my morning devotional, it gives me a chance to feel released of any negative worries and doubts that creep into my mind before the day has started. Sometimes I don't even know I am feeling a certain way or thinking about something until I've written it down. After a while things just started flowing out of you, and you start to realize patterns in your thinking that began from years past. I started to notice a pattern in the things that make me anxious; a lot of them stem from a fear of not being good enough. Having identified that from my journaling, I now have the understanding to go back and figure out how that thought got conditioned into my thinking in the first place. If not for journaling, my thoughts would never have had a chance to get out of my head.

Girl, boy—get out of your head! Write down what's on your heart, on your mind, then at least you have something to go back to when you're feeling confused about what exactly you feel or how you want to go about confronting it. Every morning do your 5p2p. Grab a pen and paper, and just write for five minutes. You all have five minutes, I promise you. If you think you don't, get up earlier, or go to bed later. It's only five minutes, but it could save you incredible amounts of time spend on overthinking and stressing.

If you cannot think of what to write about (i.e., you have absolutely no personal problems going on in your life right now), write about what you are grateful for. Write about who your best self is in your eyes. Write about where you want to be in ten years. Write about the one goal you would accomplish if you knew you could not fail. Write what's in your heart, and your mind will become clear.

You must be your own release. Release that water out of the bottle. Give your arm a break. When you're faced with anything in life—whether it's as big as heartbreak, foreclosure, death, infidelity, divorce, or debt or it's the trivial things like someone cutting you off in traffic, coming home to a messy house, your mom forgetting to pick you up on time, or your partner forgetting their piece of the presentation—*release* whatever you are feeling as a result of that situation. If you do not, it will become a growing weight on you and your heart. You could miss out on many amazing things in the future if you don't confront the pain you are feeling in this very moment.

Now let me just say, after my college boyfriend broke up with me, this wasn't exactly clear as day to me. It didn't really hit me until the following summer (a few *months* after the breakup) that I had some serious confrontation to take care of. I needed to get really clear on where all my insecurity was coming from and what I was so terrified of experiencing.

I realized that my greatest fear for relationships is fear of loss. I am so scared of giving my heart to someone and then losing them (like I did in high school) that I subconsciously decided it was better to be "halfway" in a relationship, save half of my heart, so that when I do lose them (which I figured I most certainly would at some point because all relationships end), it would only hurt half as bad. Confronting this was not easy, to say the least. Even while I'm saying it out loud and writing about it now, it makes me feel pathetic and negative. To go into a situation with the mind-set that I've already lost something before I have even given myself a chance to obtain it, is a recipe for failure.

Thing is, after confronting this fear of loss that I didn't even realize I had buried so deeply inside of me, I've been able to start releasing that fear. I am still light-years away from where I want to be, but that is the journey of personal growth. I now understand that when I am sensing that fear of loss creeping inside me, I need to remind myself of my strength. I have given my heart to people before, had it broken, *and survived*. Not only survived but become a better, stronger person because of it. The most beautiful thing in the world is a broken heart that continues to constantly give more and more love despite its fears and pains.

I understand just how strong my heart is. I've been through so much heartbreak and still continue to love as many people as I can each and every day; that is strength. I also understand that every time something breaks your heart, it is God putting something in your life to open your heart. How can you understand truly just how much love you can give and receive, if you don't put yourself in an intimate opportunity to give and receive love? You can't.

From here on out I *choose* to release my fear of loss, one little bit of confrontation at a time. For future relationships, I am going to look at them as opportunities to have divine–human connection. Through the heartbreak each one may bring, it is just another opportunity for my heart to open more and more.

Are you holding back from pain? Are fears buried inside you that you haven't explored because they are too painful or confusing or cause you too much vulnerability? I bet there is. In fact, I bet the moment you read that question there was that little something that popped into the back of your mind. Whether it's a fear of rejection because you never felt good enough for your parents, a fear of commitment because no one ever truly committed to you, a fear of loneliness because growing up you didn't have as many friends as you wanted or maybe you were even bullied—whatever it may be, confront it.

No, it isn't easy, and no, it may not seem like a pressing matter at the moment, but trust me, *it is.* Just as the water bottle didn't seem heavy at first but over time got heavier and heavier, if you continue to carry these fears buried inside you, they will get heavier on your heart, and they will continue to show up in your life until you confront them. Don't deprive yourself of living out your best life and becoming your best you because you are afraid of confronting the pain.

Identify it. Confront it. Release it.

TAKE NOTE:

1. Let go of the water bottle of life—your buried stress, pain, and anxiety. Do this by committing to the practices mentioned.
2. Meditate for at least five minutes a day. Focus on your breathing, and if you find that too difficult, just sit in a comfortable position, close your eyes, and start thinking about all the things that bring you immense joy and gratitude. Just focus on those things, If you feel your mind wandering, do not get irritated, but simply guide it back to focusing on your breathing or the things that make you happiest.
3. Practice gratitude by making a list of at least seven things you're grateful for each night. Finishing your day off with this will improve your sleep, the mood you're in when you go to sleep, and

the mood you're in when you wake up. These items can be big sources of gratitude such as *someone gave me ten million dollars today*, or little things like *the feeling of my Ugg slippers after I just get out of the shower.*

4. Journal every single day for at least five minutes. It's your 5p2p, you guys! Make it a necessity. Write about what's on your heart at the moment. Did you just go through a tough breakup? Did your mom get mad at you? Did your friend bail on you to go out with other friends and make you upset? Why did this make you feel the way you did? Explore that. That is what is going to lead you to answers about the patterns of thought that govern your everyday actions (and reactions). Once you know them, you can release them if they are not helpful. If nothing is weighing heavy on you at the moment, write about your fears, your dreams, your ideal self, anything that helps you identify key components of yourself that make up who you are today and why you do the things you do, fear the things you fear, and feel the way you do.

CHAPTER 14

Be Your Own Ego Crusher

Ego (*noun*):

1. a person's sense of self-esteem or self-importance.
2. PSYCHOANALYSIS—the part of the mind that mediates between the conscious and the unconscious and is responsible for reality testing and a sense of personal identity.
3. PHILOSOPHY—(in metaphysics) a conscious thinking subject.

My whole life I've never really considered myself an egotistical thinker. I never was way too cocky or thought that I was all that and a bag of chips. In fact, my attitude was quite the opposite, I fumed with insecurity. I was always afraid I was not good enough, not performing well enough, not pretty enough, not skinny enough—literally not anything that qualified me to be "enough." I never felt as though I reached it.

If I was ever feeling like everyone was thinking about me and what I was doing, wearing, saying, feeling, or looking like, I would just make sure that whatever they perceived me to be in that moment was *perfect*. I strived for perfection, and not just with my looks but with my clothes, my tennis record, my studies, my extracurriculars, and even my personality. I wanted to be the happiest person in every room not because I wanted that for myself, but because I wanted people to *perceive* me that way. I could care less about if I actually felt genuine happiness; I just wanted people to think I did.

This constant cycle of worrying about what other people think dominated my early teenage years and is something I still struggle with today. I don't think people ever truly rid themselves of caring about what other people think. Instead, those who seem to have overcome it have just practiced diminishing their ego so much that they've built up an ability to recognize when their ego is acting and resist it. They have realized that there is a deeper connection and meaning to life when you care more about what *you* think before other people.

Many people perceive ego as cockiness because our society has made ego out to be that way. Ego is those guys at the gym in their muscle tanks and beat headphones with muscles the size of miniature continents lifting weights equivalent to that of a small naval ship. Ego is the girl who struts her stuff around with her diamond earrings, face full of makeup, flirting with anything in sight, posting Instagrams all the time, because she *knows* she's hot stuff. Ego is this thing that only the "flashy" and "popular" and "successful" have, right? *Wrong.*

There are two types of ego, and most of us suffer from the second type without even realizing it. The second type of ego is the ego of our insecurities. How many times have you not done something because you were too afraid of what other people might think? Too afraid of what they'd say and how they'd react? More times than you can count, I'm sure; it's the same way with me. This is your ego. When we think people out there in the world actually give two rats' asses about what we are doing, wearing, or saying, how we are looking or where we are going—that is ego. When you're too afraid to do something because you're too concerned with what others will say, that is your ego taking control. It screams that "You must be such an important person that everyone is looking at you, so if you do this thing, *everyone* will see it, and your life will be over." Even if your heart pulls you toward that job, that business, those products, that relationship, or that vacation, your ego can and will pull you out of that opportunity because of insecurity.

That really is what ego is made up of: *steaming insecurity.* Whether it is your external ego causing you to flash around your muscles, newest handbag, greatest achievements, yearly salary, big house, or fancy car *or* your internal ego preventing you from living the life of your dreams because you think everyone is spending every minute of their day watching everything you do and criticizing it—it all stems from this insecurity that we are not enough as we are.

This was a game changer for me. I went from thinking I was the *least* egotistical person on the planet—never bragging about my accomplishments, never flashing around my good grades, clothes, running times, tennis records, business successes, or money earned, etc.—to understanding that, holy cow, my internal ego (the one where we think everyone is constantly thinking of us) was absolutely flaming. When I saw this, it completely redirected my intentions on how I wanted to live each and every single day. I came to realize that in order to be my happiest, I had to confront and defeat my ego. I had to let go of any steaming insecurity in my groundwork in order to build my strongest self.

Now, this hasn't been easy. In fact, this has been one of the hardest ventures I have ever embarked on. Each day, any moment I feel my internal ego start to rise where I am fearing what others think of me, I mutter "No ego" to myself over and over. This repeated self-talk, as I mentioned previously, has helped me recognize that I am in control over what I say to myself and thus what actions and thoughts I allow to proceed. This has conditioned my brain to release that egotistical insecurity that I am someone people are always giving their time and energy into judging, thinking about, and criticizing. It brings me back down to earth to help me comprehend that no, people do not waste their time and energy on judging me nearly as much as I make them out to simply because

1. They have their own life going on that is completely consuming them and their thoughts.
2. If for some reason they are thinking about me, they are thinking about me in reference to their life and their perspective, which again has nothing to do with me but everything to do with how they are fitting me into the personalized lens they are peering through.

I remember the first time my college boyfriend came to watch me play tennis. Man oh man, I was a nervous wreck. We were in that "between" phase of dating, you know, where we were talking but not official yet, and I badly wanted him to perceive me as this phenomenal athlete. I was dead set on playing well for him that day. It was also the first tournament my parents had come watch me play in since I'd gotten to college, so for me the pressure was on that day to kick some booty. I remember not being able to feel my legs, I was so nervous. I was shaking like a scared little pup.

Physically, I was on the tennis court, in my tennis uniform, holding my tennis racket, playing with a tennis ball. Emotionally, I was anywhere but the tennis court. Emotionally, I was the girl who wanted to prove to this guy she had a huge crush on that she was a boss. Mentally, I was the daughter who wanted her hard work to show off for her parents who had finally made it up to Wofford to see her play. Emotionally, my internal ego was having a freaking rave.

See, in my head my college boyfriend's mind and my parent's mind were all thinking about how well I was or was not playing. In my mind, their pride and how much they cared for me depended on whether I won or lost and whether I looked good doing it. That was my internal ego flaming right there. My internal ego was telling me, *I am so important and I have such a toll on the minds of these people that all their thoughts are on me and how I perform on this tennis court in this match*. I thought that eventually their thoughts about me were then going to affect their emotions and feelings on how much they loved me.

This raving internal ego of mine led my external ego to grow as well. I started playing *horribly* because my focus was not on how to play the tennis match but how to make sure my parents and my college boyfriend were proud of me up there. My horrible performance led me to start acting like I had no idea why this wasn't working. I had no idea why I was playing horribly, as if this was something that *never* happened and I was "so much better than this." I'm sure you've had moments like this too.

Because I let my internal ego grow like it did, I lost control of it, and it led to my external ego showing. I became flashier on the court, starting to go for winners I absolutely could not make and then freaking out when I missed them. This all stemmed from that underlying egotistical insecurity of fearing what others were thinking about me.

The reality is that my mama, dad, and even that guy at the time couldn't have cared less if I went out there and played like Roger Federer or whiffed every shot. What they cared about was whether I was happy out there playing and having fun or not. Why? Because if I was happy, *they* were happy.

When people think about others, it is naturally all in relation to *themselves*. Now you could say this is a selfish thing, but it is also our biology. We think of others in relation to our own life. So while your internal ego over there, filled to the brim with insecurity and fear of what others are thinking about you, is preventing you from living your fullest life and choosing to be a part of opportunities that fuel your soul, remember that people are thinking about you way less than you think they are. They have their own worries, problems, and life to be tending to. Yes, even your mom and dad, who would give their life for you, still think about you in regard to their own life. Only because that's all we know how to do.

You have the ability to crush your own ego. Choose to ground yourself back to earth by reminding yourself that people simply do not give you enough importance to let you be the one thing they are constantly judging, criticizing, and thinking about. People are way too busy thinking about their own lives. That thing you did or want to do that you fear so many people are going to be judging you for—honey, please. They have their own lives to worry about. They may spend two seconds thinking about that thing you did, and then they're on to the next thing in their life. So if they are spending about two seconds thinking about that thing you do, why are you spending months or years thinking about what they thought about for two seconds?

It's time to stop letting your internal ego stop you from doing things you feel are tugging on your heart for you to do. Each time you feel that fear creeping up of what people are going to think about you, repeat to yourself, "No ego, no ego, no ego."

TAKE NOTE:

1. First step is awareness. Know when your internal ego (the part of you thinking that you consume everyone else's thoughts) is running the show. A good indication of this is when you notice your external ego becomes more present. Your mood changes, and you become more flashy, bold, or cocky. Your *she-go* comes out, as I have heard before.

2. After identifying that your ego is running the show, find a phrase you can repeat to remind yourself that no one is truly thinking about you and what you're doing as much as you think they are. They might for a few seconds, but then they forget it and are on to focusing on the next thing in their own life. I say to myself, "No ego, no ego, no ego" and also write it on my hand. Find your phrase, and repeat, repeat, repeat, until it is ingrained.

3. The best way to counter ego is to immerse yourself in a serving situation—something that reminds you there are way bigger things going on in life than your fear of everyone thinking your Instagram caption was too "feministic," people thinking your new haircut is too "butch." the kids in your bio class thinking you're stupid because you're an arts major. Find something bigger than you to get involved in to remind you the world has far greater things to worry about. Go volunteer, or even better, reach out to someone you haven't had a serious conversation with in a while and make it so when y'all meet up, you talk about *them*. Other people have lives too! Talking to someone about only them helps you realize that other people are going through things, and the world really isn't looking at you as intently as you think it is. Whenever I feel my ego has been acting up, I ask wonderful people I am not super close with to go on a walk, and I make it an intention to talk about them. Ask them questions, see what is weighing heavy on their heart, and dive into their worries, loves, and fears. This takes you out of the "me, me, me" mind-set and gives your ego a knock.

CHAPTER 15

Be Your Own Joy

I feel like at the end of everyone's life, we all want one thing. We all want to look back and say we lived a happy, joyful life, one filled to the brim with love, hope, dreams that came true, family, enough money to get by comfortably, good health, and maybe an awesome pet or two.

I feel like everyone perceives joy as this thing that we all desire and crave, yet it is something out of our control. Joy is fleeting or inconsistent. It comes in with the tide every so often, just to wash away again when we're least expecting it.

I've learned a few things about this so-called sense of joy in my lifetime. Now you may be thinking, *Um, you're only twenty years old. You may think you know a lot about joy, but honey, you have yet to live a quarter of a century.* You wouldn't be wrong at all. However, I am very close with someone who is much older and much wiser than me. The lessons she taught me about joy have permeated my life and completely dictated how I live out every one of my day-to-day actions, encounters, relationships, and thoughts.

This woman is who I dedicated this book to. She is the light of my life, the absolute treasure of my heart, and one of the main reasons I am the person I am today. When you look into her eyes, you truly see light and Jesus. She is selfless, loving, and constantly pouring into people. Gwen Edmundson, along with my remarkable parents, helped raised my siblings and me when we were growing up. Gwen is in her early seventies now and has experienced more heartbreak, deceit, and pain in life than anyone whose story I have ever had the blessing of hearing. She faced abuse, raising children on her own, money scarcity, deathly illness, and unfair accusations that led to pressing court trials, and yet she is the most joyful woman I know.

She always had this saying: "I am just not going to let this steal my joy." Every time I was upset, she would say this to me and remind me that no matter what the situation is, I am always the one who controls my joy. Gwenny did not really open up to us much about her tough past until we were older. Looking back, the problems I came to her about must've seemed absolutely trivial compared to what she had gone through. I came to her about my boyfriend not texting me, my test being too hard, the blisters on my foot hurting, or that zit on my forehead growing. Instead of diminishing my worries and problems, she simply always said to tell myself in *any* situation, "I'm just not going to let this steal my joy."

This has carried me through much of my life. Though I always said this to myself, I never really put it into practice and felt it in my heart when I said it until this very year. My junior year in college is when I've finally started to realize what Gwenny was really talking about all along. See, in life people let external circumstances define their joy. They got a good grade on a test, woohoo! Joy! Joy! Joy! Their new sneakers just came in, yes! Time to be joyful! Or that girl they've been way too chicken to ask out on a date finally asked *them* out on a date—it's time to celebrate! So much joy!

Those are things to be joyful about, absolutely. However, that is also where the problem lies. That is why people see joy as this fleeting thing that comes and goes all the time because they tie it to their external circumstances. Your external circumstances are not going to be good all the time. They are not going to be positive, uplifting, or going exactly your way all the time, thus making your joy circumstantial if you tie it to how your external world is going.

The secret to lifelong happiness and fulfillment is *consistent* joy. This is what Gwenny was trying to teach me my whole life. Joy is in an internal value that you choose to have. You are always in control of how you perceive a situation; thus you can selectively decide to see the situation as one that enables growth or self-destruction. You can be in the suckiest of situations and still choose joy. You can be in the hardest of times and still choose to see the growth opportunity. Now I know there are some moments of absolutely incredible, gut-wrenching heartbreak and you may not feel joyful; I'm not telling you to. What I am saying is that on a day-to-day basis, allow gratitude to fuel your joy. You can be sad and be grateful at the same time. This gratitude will help you overcome that sadness and find more joy.

Instead of getting up every day and just going through the motions, find things to be grateful for. Stir that internal fuel of gratitude to help you find joy throughout your day. You had a bad practice? A bad test grade? A bad work presentation? No need to ruin the rest of your day with a sour attitude. Find gratitude, and that will lead you to joy. I mentioned this previously, but I want to be more granular about what you can be grateful for. You made it through the practice; be grateful. You have the opportunity to go to school, get an education, and get tested on the material; be grateful. You have a job that gives you money to provide for yourself and your family; be grateful.

By finding the gratitude, you will find the treasure in the situation. There is treasure in every little thing that happens in your life; sometimes it might just be buried a little deeper than you think it should be. So do not think for one second that your external circumstances dictate your joy. You are your own joy generator, and the fuel to this joy generator is gratitude.

I want to touch on active gratitude for a second. This is really going to get you out of your comfort zone if the rest of the practices in this book haven't already. Active gratitude is the outward action of giving back grace and appreciation. It isn't simply thinking to yourself, *I really appreciate my girlfriend Lexie taking out the trash this time*, and not doing anything else about it. Active gratitude is *telling Lexie that*. It is when you're standing in a grocery line that's a mile long thinking to yourself how busy you are and how inconvenient this line is, and you interrupt your thoughts to find the gratitude in the situation and not only think to yourself, *At least I get to stand here with my friends and spend time with them*, but also tell them that.

Oh yes, I told you guys, this is going to get uncomfortable. I'm sure some of you just thought to yourself, *Annie that would be so* weird. *In fact, some of my friends would probably ask if I was feeling all right if I told them I was grateful for them while standing in the line at Food City*. I'm telling you, active gratitude is the antidote to anxiety, nervousness, frustration, and irritation. It holds you accountable not only to generate gratitude but to express it. Expressing it is what catapults your state back into a more harmonious and centered sentiment of joy.

You want to increase the amount of joy you have in your life? Don't just find gratitude in situations, but show it to other people. Say aloud the things you find yourself dancing, giggling, smiling, and laughing about, the things that light your soul up when nothing but rain is flooding down all around you. *Express it to others*. This will bring any situation you find yourself down in back to joy.

My GwennyGwen is currently really sick. She has been struggling with scar tissue filling her lungs for the past several years, making it hard for her to breathe. I call Gwenny every day. Hearing her voice is important to me and for my heart. Amid all the turmoil of this illness, she has never once put herself down with her words. Anytime I ask how she is, even if it's a bad day and I can tell by the lack of energy in her voice, she'll say "I'm doing just great. How are you today, my sweet Annie?" Gwenny finds gratitude in everything that she does. She understands that love, grace, and joy are everything.

I remember one night this past summer, talking to Gwen about everything over cranberry juice and turkey Jersey Mikes subs, when she told me something I'll never forget. I asked her how she was doing and how she's been feeling throughout this whole experience; she had recently just had to go into the hospital overnight again because fluid filled her lungs to a dangerous degree. Gwenny's response was something I wasn't expecting but should have been. I guess I was expecting her to talk about how tired she'd been, how exhausting this whole process had been, or how sick she was of having to stay inside all the time because she isn't allowed to go outdoors. Instead, she talked of how incredible her family has been. Throughout this entire experience, though it has been so taxing on her, it has reminded her just how loved and blessed she is to have us, her family, by her side every step of the way.

Hence I said she *talked* about the many incredible blessings in her life. She didn't just think about them to cheer herself up; she *told* me about them. She *spoke* to me the gratitude she was feeling in her heart. That is one hell of a woman right there. She is one loving machine. She can find the joy in everything because she can find something to be grateful for in anything and actively express it to those around her, not just keep it all bottled up inside. She spreads her gratitude on to us each and every day by making sure we know how much we mean to her. I don't think I've ever ended a phone call without her saying "I love you, my Annie" at least three times. She understands how hard her situation is; after all, she's the one experiencing it. Yet she is also the one to find the most joy in this process because she is finding so many things to be grateful for in the midst of the turmoil and sharing them with others.

Diamonds are known to always have that shine. However, when they're first found, diamonds are in rust. That doesn't degrade their quality or significance; if anything, it makes them shine that much more brightly. Joy is like the diamond of our lives. It can shine in the good *or* the bad, if we choose it to. If we seek out the shine, then the shine will show. Gratitude is like the magnifying glass that can find even the smallest of diamonds. By choosing to be grateful, we can move ourselves toward joy even in the most heartbreaking situations. Choosing gratitude and actively expressing it, even when it may seem awkward and uncomfortable at first, almost guarantees the generation of joy.

Hear me when I say you will feel joy when you make others feel appreciated. You will feel joy when you spread what you are grateful for onto other people. You will feel joy when you shine light in a dark situation onto not just yourself but someone else. I am not saying don't feel sad if you are sad; it is vitally important to feel what you feel. What I am saying, though, is that even in sadness you can be grateful for something. Even in anger you can be grateful for something. Even in absolute chaos, turmoil, and utter frustration you can find something to be grateful for; simply having a breath in your lungs and a beat in your heart is something to be immensely grateful for. By choosing gratitude even in the hardest of times and deciding to express it for others to feel, you are choosing the path toward a more joyous direction. You are choosing healing, peace, and love.

Gwen could be mad at the world right now. Mad at God. Mad at the universe for giving her what she has. Her condition is similar to that of someone who severely struggled with smoking, yet she never smoked a day in her life. She could be telling herself, "Why me? Why is this happening to ME?" and completely self-destruct; but she's not. She's choosing gratitude. By choosing gratitude, she is allowing joy to seep into even the deepest of cracks from the hardest of heartbreaks.

It is now, in my junior year of college, that this is really sinking in for me. I have always been a joyful person, yet I was 100 percent guilty of letting external situations dictate my joy levels. This year one of my affirmations that I say to myself each morning is "*I generate my own joy.*" This engrains into my mind that no one can take my joy away from me. If my joy is not present or not at the level it should be, I am responsible for not bringing it. If my joy is very much present and alive, I am the one responsible for allowing it to show up. Yes, things in our world can influence how happy and joyful we are, I am not saying that they can't. However, on a consistent daily basis, you are responsible for you joy. If something in my environment makes me more joyful, awesome! Icing on the cake! However, the basis of my joy in that moment is not tied to that external situation. My joy was already there; now this situation is just adding to the joy I already created for myself.

My point is that you should never let someone else or some circumstance define how joyful you are. People, things, and places will always come and go. The only thing that is ensured to be constant throughout your entire life is you. That is why it is so crucial that you generate your own joy in your life. Once you stop letting surrounding things determine how happy you are each day, you can finally embrace the joy that is inside you. By conditioning your mind to find gratitude in every situation, you allow that joy to seep in whether you are aware of it or not.

Let joy heal you. Generate your own joy. The world does not determine the joy that is inside you. Joy is not fleeting or circumstantial unless you choose to base it on your circumstances. Get up each day, and be grateful to breathe, laugh, see, hear, move, and love! Someone once wrote that if the sunset happened only every ten years, then on that day everyone in the whole world would stop what they were doing, probably make a huge event out of it, and watch in awe. Yet because it happens every night, we aren't grateful for it, so we don't receive much joy from it. Don't treat the miracle of your existence like the sunset. Constantly be grateful for the gifts God gave you, even in times of utter destruction. This is the secret to generating your own joy constantly throughout your life.

TAKE NOTE:

1. Joy is generated. It is not an innate or reactive emotion; instead, it is something you are responsible for. Every morning let one of

your affirmations be "I generate my own joy." Go as far as to write on your hand, notebook, agenda, wrist, or laptop stickers that you *generate your own joy*. Put this brain tattoo on everywhere for you to see so that it seeps in that if you have joy, you brought it there, and if it is not there you let it slip from your grasp. You are responsible for your own joy. Be your own joy generator.

2. To fuel joy, find what you are grateful for in any given situation. Whether it is to make an already joyous situation that much better or a lousy situation less so, or just to give a normal monotonous day a little bit more magic, gratitude fuels joy. Identify even the tiniest of things to be grateful for—a ray of sunshine, the glimmer of a spiderweb in the morning dew, the way your lavender and vanilla candle smells after you get out of the shower—and let yourself feel that gratitude well up inside you.

   The key in this practice is to *actively express* that gratitude to others. We have limitations to what we can feel as human beings; when we have an emotion, we can only feel so much of that emotion. However, when we share that emotion with other people, that emotion amplifies. When you share gratitude with others, that gratitude amplifies and leads to an even greater generation of joy. Start small; in little moments simply mention to friends how beautiful the sunset looks, how great it is to be spending time with them tonight at the movies, or how fun it is getting guacamole and queso with them at the downtown Tex-Mex. Maybe go a little deeper next time and share just how grateful you are for their love, support, and constant friendship. Gratitude fuels us on a path to joy even amid the hardest of situations, but actively expressing and sharing that gratitude with others launches us into a more joyous state almost instantaneously.

CHAPTER 16

Be Your Own Normal

My whole life I've struggled with that feeling of not fitting in. I've never felt I was doing the normal thing, acting my age, or doing whatever everyone else was doing. I always felt as if I enjoyed things that were different, bizarre, strange, and nothing like what the people surrounding me were interested in. Even now, writing this paragraph, it is around nine thirty on a Friday night at my college, and I preferred to stay in to write this chapter of the book. *This* makes me excited. *This* is fun to me.

Growing up, I was told all the time I need to let loose and have more fun—that if I kept doing what I was doing with my life, I would look back and regret not having any fun. I was so self-conscious about this growing up. I hated telling people how early I liked to get up (usually around 4:30 to 5:00 a.m.) and how early I liked to go to bed. I had endless anxiety around the fact that I hated going to parties where the music was so loud that you couldn't have real conversations with people. I'd rather stay at home with an amazing book or movie than go to a party, and this ate me alive.

I didn't understand why I couldn't be more like kids my age: go to parties, drink, flirt, dance, eat my face out with crappy food, and just enjoy it. Thing is, every time I did do this, giving into the social pressures and pretending to be like my peers and do these things every weekend, I felt like crap. I felt so out of alignment with my heart and what made me *me*. Before I set off for that party or gathering, I would always feel proud of myself because I was finally stepping up and being "normal." However, once I got there, all I could think about was how much I'd rather be reading that self-development book, getting some good sleep so I could wake up early and have a killer run, how much my body probably wanted to punch me right now for scarfing down the crappy food I'd eaten and slurping down disgusting drinks, or how emotionally drained I felt after having one drunk conversation after another with my friends who'd had a little bit too much liquid courage that night.

I was trying so hard to be normal that I never realized the power I had within myself to define my own normal. I thought something was legitimately wrong with me. I mean, come on. A twenty-year-old college student who prefers to stay in on a weekend night to better her self-development and continue writing her first book—yeah, ha-ha, totally normal. I don't say this in a condescending way, either. I'm not prancing around thinking I'm better than everyone else because I'm staying in reading on a Friday night while most kids are out there taking shots and breaking out their craziest dance moves. If that makes them happy, then that is *good* for them, and that should be their normal.

See, that is the thing so many people fail to understand. People will spend their whole entire lives looking at the crowd for what should be their normal. They look at other people for cues as to how they should act, dress, speak, think, live, and even love. That understanding should not come from anyone but yourself. If you define the way you live by the societal normal of how everyone else is living their lives, your actions will support the lifestyle that makes *them* happy, not yourself. You must take a second, stop, breathe, and really think about what makes *you* happy. Not your friends, not your parents, not your siblings, your teachers, your coaches … but just you. What does living into your happiest lifestyle look like?

I did a lot of reflection on this recently before starting my junior year at Wofford. In the past, I was awfully insecure about the fact that I have never been a huge partygoer—and when I say that, it doesn't mean that I have anything against those who love parties at all! Being in college has completely highlighted this insecurity, especially since the most prominent stereotype of college is that it is just four crazy years of partying.

Before this year of college, I really reflected on what made me happiest. I realized that I am my happiest when I have spent my days fully connecting with people—having real, immense, thoughtful conversations that promote openness to new ideas, perspectives, and deeper connections.

At night I love to have my me time. I love to read my self-development books, write in my journal, or watch Planet Earth documentaries. Yes, this sounds completely dorky! Trust me, for years I struggled with this part of me that I just couldn't shake. I wanted so badly to be the girl who lived for the weekends and was excited to go to parties to drink and dance. And that's not to say I never go out because I totally do at times! However, instead of pushing down that nudge in me that was saying *This isn't you* or *This isn't your normal* every time I tried to be someone I wasn't, I listened to it and acted on it.

Time for the specifics because what is all this mumbo jumbo motivation without any practices for implementation? It is awesome to get fired up, you guys, and I hope this book is doing that for you so far, but I wanted to reiterate that knowledge is simply potential power. It is one thing to know all these principles and have them stored in your brain for an instant as you read them to make you feel empowered and better about yourself; it is a whole other ball game for you to actually execute and act on that knowledge. That is the power and magic in knowledge: it isn't the means of it stored in your brain but the implementation of it—turning it into action in your everyday life.

Do these practices. Yes, I know you have teachers, coaches, parents, friends, bosses, spouses, and others telling you to do things you don't want to do. However, I'm not telling you to do these practices for selfish purposes; I want you to do it for *you*. You will not gain from this book as you could unless you implement these practices in your life. *Every single one.*

This one's good, so hold on to your bootstraps. It's one of my favorites that I've ever done, and no, unlike some of the others, it isn't something you have to devote time to every single day or put a reminder for it on your phone. This is something you can only do once if you do it strongly, directly, and honestly enough. You may find, though, that after doing this once, you will want to do it again eventually when your life shifts direction once again (which is inevitable).

I want you to write a letter to yourself, a letter that lets out every single part of you—your fears, worries, desires, dreams, strengths, weaknesses, hopes, struggles … all the stuff that maybe you've been ignoring for a little too long. You guys, I want this to be emotional. I want you to let out everything onto this paper, as if you got a chance to talk to your life and let out everything and anything you'd say to it.

After you've let out all the frustrations, I want you to write about your best self. Who is your best self? Here's the trick: it doesn't have to be based on the capabilities of the person you are today. Write as if you had a blank slate of life in front of you, free from any past mistakes, accomplishments, and reputations. Write down who your best self would be if you could choose any combination of traits in the world. You're honest, kind, compassionate? Write down where your best self would be. Would you be living in Fiji, Colorado, or Toronto? Write down who's in your life. That super-hot checkout guy from Target is your husband? You have four children? Your parents live an hour and a half away—not too close but not too far? Write it all down.

Next I want you to write down the answer to this question: What makes you happy as that best version of you? Split it up into weekdays and weekends because those seem to be distinctly different for most of us. Are you getting up at 5:00 a.m. and working out, then going to class, eating three healthy meals a day, and coming home at night to watch Netflix to cool down? Are you getting up early to read, eating six small meals a day, working out at night, and then journaling before bed? On the weekends do you get up early to work out and then go enjoy your day with your friends at the darty (day party)? Or do you opt for brunch with your friends, work out in the afternoon, and spend the night listening to podcasts and catching up on some self-development reading? Write it down. Once you've identified what makes you happiest as the best version of yourself, you will stop apologizing for it. Way too often we fall prey to acting on what others think is best for us simply because we haven't taken the time to define our boundaries and pursue the things that fill us up.

For my party people tonight, if that is where you find your deepest connections, highest spirit, and happiest self, go dance your ass off! For my stay-in people (like myself), if reading that book, watching that TV show, doing that workout, or trying that new recipe is instead what fills you up on your Friday nights, do that! Do it unapologetically. Only you have the power to define what is normal in your life. That is because only you truly can connect deep within yourself to know what is best for you and what makes you happiest. Conforming and changing yourself to fit the societal standards of everyone else who says what you're supposed to be doing, is like pouring the foundation of a house that won't support your own destined lifestyle. It's more like building your house on the sand. If you build it with inconsistent, unaligned, inadequate values, principles, and experiences, your house (or the lifestyle that you are building yourself) will never stay strong against the constantly shifting weather conditions. However, if you build your house with brick—strong, aligned, sturdy structural material—your house will stand up against even the thickest of storms.

I also am a huge runner—I mean *big-time* runner. Now you may say, "Annie, this isn't abnormal. I know a ton of people who love to run." That is entirely true, and I'm sure they run a lot more than I do. However last year my running really picked up, to the point where people started noticing it. I became known as that tennis player who runs all the time. Even the security guards would crack jokes that the one person on campus they wouldn't have to ever go catch is me because I'd just run away from them. Granted, Wofford has around fifteen hundred students (if that), so it isn't hard to develop a reputation for yourself if you start doing something consistently overtime.

I'd get up at 4:30 a.m., run six miles, have practice (sometimes conditioning and weights too), and I was getting in ten miles on practice days, four miles on match days, and twelve to fourteen miles on off days. This was my running schedule, and I *loved* every single little bit of it. Maybe it's because most people look at running as a punishment, something that hurts and causes pain, that they didn't understand my love for it or why I was constantly doing it.

To me running is therapy. It clears my heart, soul, and mind. It is where I develop my greatest confidence and learn my greatest lessons. I listen to so many podcasts and sermons on my runs (and your occasional Bon Jovi) that I always feel connected to the Lord during them. It creates this internal bliss like nothing else, a happiness that reaches uncharted limits within my soul.

Of course, did anyone ever ask me all this before they judged how much I ran? Nope, they just judged. I'm sure many thought it was some form of exercise bulimia, some thought it was my way of running away from the hard college breakup I had just gone through, and some thought

I was just OCD and couldn't get off "the grind." This was the first time in my life I knew I wasn't doing the "normal"; I knew it made people uncomfortable, and I knew that people were talking about it behind my back, yet I kept *going*. Why? Because it made me happy! I was not about to sacrifice one of the most incredible things in my life for people who did not care enough about me to ask me why I did it before they started judging. Running lifted my spirits, made me confront my deepest and darkest thoughts, and grew me as a person. I am eternally grateful for it. In spite of the sly remarks from my coach, teammates, friends, and other members of the Wofford community, I knew deep in my heart that this was something that generated happiness for me. It wasn't normal, no. Yet it was *my* normal. In order to be my best self, I needed this to be something in my normal.

Identify what makes you *you*—what makes you happy, fills you up, lifts your spirits—and allow yourself to accept that as your normal. It doesn't have to be your neighbor's normal or your pet's, friend's, boyfriend's, or girlfriend's; nope, just yours. After coming to this realization and clarifying that things like getting up before dawn, reading at night, listening to podcasts instead of the newest pop music, being more interested in writing a novel and growing my business than my actual college classes, and running my butt off every day even though long distance is super bad for tennis (works the long twitch muscles instead of the fast twitch muscles) make me my happiest self, I understood the importance of making this my normal—and not stopping there, but actively fighting this urge in me that did not want this to be my normal, the urge that wanted me to be that twenty-year-old college girl, not worried about the real world yet and up to date with all the newest songs, who loved to go out and party on her Friday and Saturdays, only wanted to focus on her college classes and not other business ventures, and did no more than what her coach told her to do at practice (no extra running). Thing is, though, if I did all of that, I would not be happy.

Everyone comes to a point of realizing that their happiness is what truly matters. The problem is, most of us don't reach this realization until we're like sixty or seventy years old, with all those years wasted worrying about what other people thought about us or what we were doing. We spent those years directing our actions toward living the lifestyle that creates someone else's happiness instead of creating a lifestyle that makes for our own happiness. You can change this. You can save all those years.

I realized this before I came into school this year. I could spend the rest of my college experience up to my ears in anxiety about what people thought of how early I got up, my excessive running, my business, my book in the making, the fact that I like to stay in on weekend nights and read—or I could own all that. It makes me happy; why in the world would I stop doing what makes me happy in order to please someone who truly doesn't even care that much about what I'm doing in the first place?

Does my staying in affect the people who want to go out? Absolutely not. Does my running, business, book, or self-development reading hurt anyone? Negative. Even though my pursuits hurt no one and make me my happiest self, I'd be willing to throw them away to live out a lifestyle that doesn't make me happy and no one seems to care about? Doesn't make sense, right? Why would you throw away the things that build your spirits in the long term to "fit in" for a temporary, fleeting moment in the short term? Doesn't make sense, yet we this is what we do!

We let society define our "normal." We let it dictate our thoughts, feelings, actions, and behaviors, and if what we feel in our hearts doesn't align with the societal standards, boy oh boy, then something is wrong with us! *This is not the truth!* You can redefine your "normal" and live into your best life that way.

Someone once told me a rocket ship uses about 70 percent more of its fuel in the first sixty seconds after launch than it does in the rest of its whole journey because the force of gravity is greatest in those first sixty seconds. In a way, this is a lot like life. When we are first starting to define our "normal"— doing the do of what we are most passionate about, laying the groundwork for a life of our dreams—*that* is when we need to use up most of our fuel; *that* is when most people are going to try to pull us down, much like the force of gravity trying to pull down that rocket ship.

My friend, whether you are just now embarking on your journey of self-love, passion, and carefree bliss, have been on it for a while now, or have already established a firm foundation for a life you can truly call your own—always remember: when people try to pull you down, *you are that rocket ship.* Do not let the gravitational pull of societal standards keep you from skyrocketing into unknown, magical realms beyond most people's reach. Define what makes you happiest. Identify the routines, principles, values, and daily behaviors you follow when you are your best self, and live into that. Be your own normal. Do not let society determine the foundation of the lifestyle you are cultivating for yourself.

TAKE NOTE:

1. Write yourself a "Dear my best self" letter; just do it. You need to identify what it is that makes you happy while being the best version of yourself. Not what makes your coach happy, your team happy, your mom happy, your professor happy, your sister or friend or roommate or suitemate or boyfriend or girlfriend happy, but you.

2. Dear My Best Self … start by getting out all the frustrations you have in life. You will not be able to get to a place of utmost inner peace to identify your best you if you have all these weights on your heart. These weights are your past, your mistakes, shame, disappointment, misery, failure, ego—the list could go on and on. Release it onto the paper. Get mad. Get scared. Cry. Let it out.

3. Think about your best you, and write about it. How do you respond in times of chaos? Who are you with? Where are you living? What brand yoga pants do you wear? Is your hair short or long? What is heavy on your heart? Where do you find your inner peace? What makes your light shine? The more specific this is, the better. Hell, in my letter I specified what kind of dog I want in the future as my best self (can't wait for Winston, my goldendoodle pup, to come into my life!). The more specific, the more real, and thus the more obtainable your brain deems it to be.

4. Write down what makes your best self happy. Write down the schedules your best self follows to be his or her best. Yes, I am aware life can be hectic, and no schedule is guaranteed to be set in stone every day for the rest of your life, but what are the major activities that are *nonnegotiables* in the schedule of your best self? For example, my morning cup of coffee, devotional, 5p2p minutes,

and workout are nonnegotiable. I know in order to be my best self each day, any day, I must do those things. What are those things for you? Write them in the letter.

5. All those things I just wrote above, just do them.

CHAPTER 17

Be Your Own Now

The other day I was at a funeral service for a dear friend of mine who passed away this summer. Dr. John Pilley was, as some would say, the absolutely GOAT (greatest of all time) in his day.

The first time we met, I was on the treadmill in the Wofford gym at 5:00 a.m. as always, and an older gentleman (I later found out he was in his early nineties) came up to me and asked me what my mythological character was. It was one of those moments when someone says something so off the wall that you're like "Huh? My mythological who?" *What is this dude on?* I was super taken aback at first, not because I was partially winded from juggling the sprint workout I was doing in the moment, not falling off the treadmill going at thirteen miles an hour, and trying to talk to this man, but also because that wasn't your everyday "Let me strike up a convo" kind of question.

After I got to know Dr. Pilley better, looking back, I wasn't surprised at all that he would come up and ask me a question like that out of the blue. He was my gym buddy. We were the only ones in the gym at four thirty in the morning, and we became quite good friends. He loved to see the world, so every morning I would set up his treadmill settings to "visual exploring"; that way the screen could take him to Venice, Rome, Brussels, Paris—anywhere he wanted to go. I loved our conversations about life and curiosities. I am a psychology major at Wofford, and he himself used to teach psychology here. He is also one of the most renowned scientists in the world for his research with dogs; his own dog became famously known as the smartest dog in the world under his own training.

I really knew Dr. Pilley for just under a year. Still, he had a major impact on the way I view life and all of its precious moments. Moments like a memorial service really make you realize how special life is. It strikes me as ironic that times of death or destruction are when people start really living the most. It is in those moments where life is in jeopardy, or life has ended, that many lives start to renew and blossom yet again.

I was thinking about this as Dr. Pilley's daughter got up to speak at this service. She shared a poem that struck a chord deep within my heart. The poem was about the dash of life—how on a tombstone it is not the two dates that matter (the birth and the death date) but the dash in between. It is what you did between those two dates that counts. Between those two dates lie the *dash*, symbolizing the love you shared in your time, the family you created, the memories you had, the lessons you learned, and the legacy you left.

No one has ever seen a U-Haul following a hearse on the way to the funeral. Why is this? Because you don't get to keep your material goods with you! All you have when you leave this very earth is the love that you shared and the legacy that you left behind. Everything else *does not matter*. It is irrelevant.

Take a second and ask yourself, what are you leaving behind? What legacy are you creating this very second? Mother Teresa once told Oprah it is impossible to know your legacy because your legacy is determined by how many people you touch and influence in this world. This is impossible to know. You cannot know just how many people you touch. You can touch someone by simply holding the door for them at a Barnes & Noble, anonymously buying the person's meal behind you in the drive thru at Chick-fil-A, or leaving an extra-large tip at the restaurant to the waitress who is working a double shift that night. You have no idea how many people you influence, but your legacy is all determined by just that. That is why every encounter, interaction, relationship, and conversation is a chance to improve, shift, change, and continue to build up your legacy.

So many of us get caught up in the trivial matters of life- I say this not as an attack on others but as a way of relating to most people: *I am totally guilty of this.* Just the other day I was frustrated because I couldn't find one song on the radio that I would enjoy listening to—not one. Then the light turned red right as I got to it. Then they didn't have my size when I went to the store to get new running shoes that I wanted so badly. Then, lo and behold (God forbid), I went to QuikTrip, and when they were out of the Extra watermelon-flavored bubble gum that I always get because it tastes like a fruity, summertime explosion in my mouth, I was irritated.

Oh yes, you guys, my irritation was at a slight high. *It happens.* Am I proud to say I got irritated by those things? No. Do I sound like a brat? Yes. Do I want to admit that to you guys? No. But it happens *all* the time. We get caught up in the daily grind and forget about what kind of legacy we are creating in the moment. We worry way too much about likes on Instagram, Snapchat story filters, what drinks we're having that night, how slim our waists are, or whether or not we're having a good hair day, instead of focusing on what are we *giving* to the world. Who are we *becoming* for the world in this very moment?

The truth is, that is all we have—*this moment.* You never know when you aren't going to have a next moment. You never know what is going to come next. In each moment when I get a chance, I always ask myself, how is my energy right now? Am I pouring into others the way I want to? Am I receiving the energy I want to be? If not, *I change it.*

Do what I call an energy check. When you find your irritation rising like a thermometer on a summer day in Hotlanta, pause. Check in with your energy. Why are you really irritated? It isn't because of the gum, the red light, or the shoe size. It's probably because your coach said something that rubbed you the wrong way earlier, or your friend wasn't there for you in the way you hoped.

Identify the source of what you are feeling in this very moment because as I learned at Dr. Pilley's service, *this* moment is truly the only guarantee we have in our life right now. That last moment, it's gone. We can't guarantee the next one. We only have this very one we are in. Why not make it the best?

Check in with yourself to see what energy you are bringing to the moment and how your energy is being affected if it isn't where you want it to be. If it isn't where you want it to be, either amp up your energy by changing your attitude—listen to something that will pump you up, talk to people who'll pour into you, journal out your frustrations, go work out to change your state—or change your environment. Get out of your car if you are getting frustrated driving around, change the blaring Kanye music to something more subtle like Ed Sheeran, read the self-development novel instead of watching the new episode of *The Bachelorette*. Whatever you do is up to you, but if your energy is not where you want to be, either change your attitude, or change your environment.

Each moment is a precious opportunity to amplify your *now*. Taking advantage of your right now is your vehicle to legendary. There is no tomorrow or yesterday in the vocabulary of the greats; there is only the now. Look around you. Embrace your environment. Smell the smells, touch your environment, breathe the air, and see the colors. Capitalize on your superpower to take advantage of your right now. Do the most with what you have in this moment—which if you have a beat in your heart and a breath in your lungs, anything can be done in this moment. Including, that next one big step being taken by you toward your dream life.

My favorite thing to do with my dad growing up was to go to graveyards. This might sound weird and strange, and to be honest, it probably is, but that's our thing. We are both huge history freaks, so anytime I had a few hours in between tennis matches during junior tournaments we'd go to these old graveyards and explore. Last year when he came up for a Wofford match, we went exploring at an old graveyard in Spartanburg afterward. Walking around the old graves, all I could think about was what the stories of these people were. I wasn't concerned with what their houses looked like, how much money they had, the clothes they wore, or even how many followers on social media they had (joking; these people were from the Civil War period).

My point is, when I was looking at the dirt that covered the bodies of these people buried feet below the ground, all that extra "fluff" that in today's society we define ourselves by—it just didn't matter. I was curious about their families. I was intrigued by their heart, soul, character, and lifestyle. I wanted to know more about the way they treated people, their community, how they served, and the impact they left. Was the world a better place because of them?

You don't have to be a Martin Luther King Jr. or a Mahatma Gandhi to change the world. Simply by being a loving, giving, gracious, and serving soul in every "now" of your days, you are changing the world for the better. Do you know how many people just need to interact with someone who is loving? Who is giving? Who cares about their thoughts, feelings, worries, and emotions? Be that for someone. Be that for yourself! If all you have right now is this very moment, make it the best damn moment you possibly can.

Define your dash. Go make your now the best there is. That is all you have, your right now, this very moment. Tomorrow isn't guaranteed, and the past cannot be changed, so accept that and just go with it. You can be whoever you want to be in this very instant. You don't like who you are? Redefine yourself. You think you can do better than you've done in the past? Make a new commitment to yourself to do better starting this moment. My dear friend Dr. Pilley left this world having touched hundreds and hundreds of lives. He always served people with a loving, open, and honest heart. He didn't have a lot of material wealth—but did that stop tons and tons of people flooding in to that memorial service? Absolutely not, because what he did have was *soul* wealth. He was rich as can be in the department of love, affection, and grace; and he gave away those riches to others constantly. That is what was mentioned in the service. Not his car, not his clothes, not even all the awards he won, but his heart of service, passion, and love that touched so many.

What legacy are you building now that will one day be the only thing you leave behind? This very moment is an opportunity to define it, manifest it, and act on it. Make the dash between the years count because a wise person once said it is not the years of your life that matter, but the life in your years. Be your own *now*.

TAKE NOTE:

- All you have is this moment. This moment, along with all the other little moments, makes up your dash which creates the legacy you are leaving behind in this world.
- Your now is made up entirely of the energy you are investing into it. Complete moment-to-moment energy checks to ensure you are giving it optimal energy.
- Energy check—Pause and ask yourself how your energy is at the moment. Is it the energy your best self would project into this

world? If so, keep it up, rock star! In fact, ask yourself, "How can I make this even better?" If it isn't where you want it to be, identify if the things you are getting irritated about are the real issue or if there is an underlying issue. Confront the underlying issue by either addressing it head-on or actively choosing to let it go.

- Once you're rid of the underlying frustration, either change your personal state by doing something that lifts you up (a walk, a jog, twenty minutes of reading, a coffee date with a friend, going to Target to smell the scented candles ... is this a regular thing for anyone else?) or change your environment. Get out of the car, out of the house, out of the office. A new change of scenery can shift your energy sometimes with no effort on your part but simply the decision to physically get up and move.

CHAPTER 18

Be Your Own Dream

When I was younger, I wanted to be a princess. My dream, specifically, was to be Sleeping Beauty. I remember being at my great-grandmama's house one night and looking up at the big sky filled with stars, praying that tomorrow I'd wake up and my dream would come true—I'd wake up as Sleeping Beauty. Now why on earth I dreamed to be the princess who slept through 85 percent of the movie, I couldn't tell you. However, that was the first time I'd ever had that magical feeling of what a dream felt like—what it felt like to want something that badly, to crave it, to let it consume your thoughts and sparkle your insides.

Now I can honestly say a little over a decade later my dreams have become a smidge more realistic in the sense that I am not dreaming of waking up to have become an animated and fictional character; yet at the same time, the essence of what my dreams make me feel have not changed. The rush of heat I get in my belly when I hear something, see something, or experience something that sparks that dream in me is all still the same as it was for that eight-year-old girl who dreamed of being Sleeping Beauty.

The next time I really felt that adrenaline in my veins, that beat explode in my heart, and that tingle in my soul, was when I was nineteen years old. I was at a conference for the physical and financial wellness company my mom had been building her business with for the past couple of years. I was sitting in the auditorium at this conference, and a young girl got up to speak. She was around twenty-seven years old, a company millionaire, and she was telling her story. Her name is Emily Vavra. When she got up and spoke (in front of thousands of people) of her abused, tormented, self-loathing past, her words sent shivers into the spines of everyone in the audience. Then she gradually gravitated toward how those experiences made her the woman she is today, the strong, compelling, successful, bold, and grateful woman standing before us. She explained how this company led her down a new path of freedom—*personal freedom*. Physically she felt better than ever, financially she had made her way slowly but surely toward financial freedom, and personally she was using her tormented past as means to make her the strongest version of herself.

Hearing this young woman speak, all I could think of was my past struggles with my eating disorder, self-hatred, insecurity, vulnerability, trust, and fear. That is when the dream was born in me. I want to use this opportunity to become nutritionally the best I can be so I can feel, act, and love the best I can; financially, I want to make more so I can give more and become the best version of myself in the process; personally, I want to lead others to do the same so they can become their best selves. This dream struck into my heart like lightning. I wanted this company to be the vehicle to carry out my dream. She ended her speech saying this company is a personal development company with wellness products and a compensation plan attached. Ever since that moment I have been ferociously pushing toward self-improvement, nutritional excellence, and financial freedom.

Sitting in those seats, I felt unstoppable. Don't we all feel that way when we first start dreaming? The opportunities are endless, right? You're going to be the quickest, the wealthiest, the fittest, the youngest at whatever your goal is, right? But then right when you buy the thing, build the page, create the scripts, find the company—fear happens. The doubt creeps in. You start doing the do, pitching your piece, and the chatter starts chiming in. When I say chatter, I don't necessarily mean other people. I mean your own chatter. What will people think of me? How am I ever going to be successful at a sales job if I can't even sell one pack in two weeks? I suck, I'm no good, I might as well quit ... yes, that's usually how our dreams come and go. We have all this momentum, fire, passion, and vision, and then *cease fire*; all of that stops immediately when doubt creeps in. Prince Ea (a famous poet) once said, "Look out for doubt, because he's under arrest for murder. He's killed more dreams than failure ever did."

We give up on our dreams way too easily, way too soon. We don't even make it to the point where people have the opportunity to push down our ideas, because *we* push them down before anyone else ever gets the chance! In fact, if people are selectively choosing to spend their own energy and time talking about your business, your book, your hobby, or your craft, whether they are supporting it or not, that means you've made it a lot farther than most dreamers. You've gone past the point where most people stop after listening to their own doubtful remarks and thoughts. So if people are talking about you, heck yes! That means you are farther along in pursuing your dreams than most people ever get.

Here's the reality of dreams; listen closely. People are not afraid to *start* their dreams. That fire, that passion, that abundant energy when new inspiration strikes does not just evaporate overnight. Most people do in fact act on their dreams at first. Why? Because that feeling is too addicting not to be acted on. Here's the thing: most people's challenge doesn't come from the fear of starting their dreams but from the fear of being seen starting *small*. People's egos are way too big. They want to have massive amounts of success, praise, money, or fame, yet they aren't willing to take the little steps and first be seen starting small (maybe even crazy) in order to eventually be seen as something extraordinary.

Y'all listen up, the light only uncovers what is done in the dark. If you do not put in the little steps, the little amount of time, do the speeches where only three people show up, do the sales pitches where only one person is interested, do the business launch parties where only two people show up (and one of them is your mom), all while getting little to no recognition for it, then you are not doing it right. None of the A players started with massive amounts of success. They all started small and were deemed crazy. The Wright Brothers? Can you imagine what people probably thought of them at the time? They were trying to *fly*, for Pete's sake, before flying was ever a thing! Their neighbors were probably including them in their prayer list at night: "Lord, please take care of the crazy folks next door who for some reason think it is sane to have humans flying in the air." I can only imagine the gossip that went on underneath. Yet in today's world, they are legendary. That is all because they weren't afraid to be seen starting small. They were willing to keep pushing through with their dream step by step, even when their egos started butting in, and kept on when other people's egos started commenting.

I presented at a sip and sample last week. Pause. You're probably wondering what the heck a sip and sample is. To be brief, it is basically an opportunity for people to come out to try some of our products and hear firsthand testimonies, transformation stories, and information about what our physical and financial wellness company can do for them. I've only spoken at one before, and it was at my grandmama's house, and I simply gave my two-minute testimony in front of a couple of elderly ladies. My mom was running most of that show, so I didn't have to do much.

However at this one, I was in charge of most of it, along with a good friend of mine, Stephanie, who is also in the company. Let me tell you—your girl was nervous. The night before, I was tossing and turning because I was so nervous to get up there and speak in front of a handful of women about the compensation plan of this company, the history, and some of the product information. In my head I ran through what I was going to say a million times. I felt ready, yet in the back of my mind were those fears: "What are they going to think of me? What if I mess up? What if I offend someone, or they mock me, scold me, think I'm too young, too this, too that …?"

I stopped that train of thought. I did what I do most of the time when I feel I am in an endless, fear-driven thought cycle: I opened up my podcast app and listened to Robin Sharma. Something he touched on that struck me before that meeting was the massive amounts of energy I expend worrying about what others are thinking of me, energy I could be spending on how I am going to think of *them*.

Instead of worrying about how others are going to perceive you, love you, or hate you, shift your focus to how you perceive them: How can you be of service to them? How can you love on them? This gets you out of that me-me-me mind-set and puts a greater cause into your mind. I realized I am there to serve others, to give others my message and speak into them this opportunity to help them, serve them, and love them. I am not there to be seen as the "perfect" girl who never messes up when she speaks, and any earlier worries about that were just my ego speaking.

I switched my mind-set from thinking of *How am I going to be seen? Is this going to help or destroy my reputation?* to *How can I see others? How can I help others?* Once I made that shift, the negative and self-doubtful thoughts didn't necessarily stop, but the volume turned way down, to the point where I felt I could really engage with my audience, pick up cues on what they needed to hear, and feel their energy to bring the energy I needed to bring for them.

Fear and doubt are probably the two worst murderers of our time. They kill dreams every day. Someone wants to start a clothing line? Fear creeps in and kills the dream. Someone dreams of being the next Victoria Secret angel? Others' belittling opinions feed their own doubt, and the dream is demolished.

Whenever you are about to do something big—giving a presentation on your new startup company, talking to your first client for your home-run business, cold calling for the first time—and you start to get all nervous, fearful, and doubtful, remember something that Oprah once said. "Nervousness is in fact a selfish emotion. It means you care more about what other people think than what you can offer them." If you believe in your dream and the services that can come from your dream, then you need to shift your focus away from your fear of what others are thinking of you and onto the opportunity that's available for you to serve them.

Serve humanity with your dream, with your craft. For our truest callings in our life are created when our heart of service meets our heart of passion. Your dreams stem from passion and come to life when they provide service to others. So stop doubting your own capabilities and start owning the ability your dream has to serve the masses of humanity.

You dream of owning a taco truck? You have the opportunity to serve people tacos that make them smile, brighten their day, and give them a service that warms their hearts and lights their souls. As a taco truck owner you can get to know your customers and make them feel important and beautiful. That is your heart of passion and heart of service coming together in creating the life of your dreams. Dreams are much more than just something about us; they are things that light up the whole world. Your dream can impact this world, make a difference, and ignite the light in others to pursue their dreams and furthermore add to our culture.

You have a seed planted inside you. That seed is passion. Your passion comes alive when it is watered with encouragement, surrounded by the right environment, and nourished with the proper materials. Listen to that passion inside you, and immerse yourself in an environment where it can grow! When we put an oak tree in the desert, we don't blame the oak tree for its inability to grow; we blame the environment. So why is it that we blame ourselves for falling short of our goals when we are immersing ourselves in environments where our growth is not possible?

Go find your proper environment with the right people and inspiration that lifts you up. Once you do, let your passion grow all around the world to make an impact, be of service, and help others in the process. That is what your calling is, to use your passion as service. Once you realize that, the fear of what others think about you, how others will react, even the fear of your own ego's opinion of yourself, will hush. The fear won't go away completely, but the volume will be turned down.

Your weakness that makes you give in to the fear of what others think will be overcome by the strength you build from the exponential expansion of your vision for helping others. Your mission to pursue your dream will have the backbone of your confidence, which stands on the fact that you know you are serving a greater purpose by living out your passion and desires.

Stop making it about you. Your dream isn't just about you! It is about something so much greater- it is about the goodness of the people in our world today. They need your heart of passion to meet your heart of service. They need your dream. They need you to live out your dream.

TAKE NOTE:

1. It is easy to catapult into a dream when you are first starting out and fall into this false pretense that everything is going to go exactly as you plan, everyone will support your vision, and basically it's just a matter of time before people are bowing down to your blue checkmark on Instagram that you acquired after becoming an overnight millionaire. Let me spread some realistic sprinkles on that idea real fast. I can almost 99.9999% guarantee you that you won't successfully achieve any dream without adversity. *All achievers faced adversity on their way to their goal.* If they didn't, their dream probably wasn't big enough to make much of an impact and get people stirring. Why is this so? Because dreams rattle lives. They shake people in all sorts of ways. If you want to

be a dreamer, and also someone who successfully goes after their dreams, prepare to be shook.

2. Go into your dream identifying how you are going to best respond to the adversity you can plan for. I said *that you can plan for* because most of our obstacles are things we never knew were coming. However, there are things that have a high statistical probability of happening—family not supporting you, your friends thinking you're crazy, not having enough money in your budget, running out of time, not having the connections or resources ... the list could go on and on.

   Whatever your dream is, however special you think it is, someone out there has had it before. Maybe it's not your exact invention, book idea, song lyric, or restaurant title, but there have been inventors before in our history. People wanted to produce award-winning movies before, musicians have had the dream to make music before, and chefs and bakers aimed to create food for the public before. Study those who succeeded at their ventures. You do not have to do all the problem solving yourself! Find out what their struggles were, and find out what they did to get through them.

   This all starts with identifying what potential problems could come your way and having a plan to combat them. You're a struggling entertainer who dreams of having her own talk show but doesn't have the money, resources, or connections? Literally go online to one of the millions of YouTube videos on Oprah. See how she did it. Study how she got through her friends not supporting her, her financial struggles, and the struggles she faced as a black woman, anything and everything you can find. *Prepare for adversity*—at least, as much of it as you can before it comes. Also remember that when obstacles rise, someone has always been through what you're going through now and gotten out of it successfully. Study what they did. If not for YouTube and "Google University," I probably would not be writing this book right now.

3. Pick the right environment for your dream to grow in. This includes but is not limited to the people, places, things, activities, behaviors, thoughts, actions, and feelings that your dream will

be growing in. For the naysayers in your life who don't believe in your dream or in your ability to accomplish it, I understand that you can't necessarily shut them out of your life, since some of them could be family, friends, or maybe even your significant other.

What you can do is "put your blinders on" to them. Limit your openness with them when it comes to conversations about your goals. There is no need to tell them about something they are going to bash and shame. Save those conversations for people who are going to nourish and help grow that dream. Hold yourself to the same standards with environments, activities, behaviors, thought patterns ... remember, you do not have to completely stop these factors but limit your dream's exposure to them. This dream is your seed, you guys. In order for it to grow to its fullest potential, you have to hold the environment you are letting it grow in to the highest standard.

CHAPTER 19

Be Your Own Forgiveness

Third grade. My three best friends at the time decided they thought it'd be funny if they didn't talk to me at recess that day to see if I'd come over and "fight for our friendship." Later, when I asked why the heck I couldn't climb the monkey bars with them, they said it was to "test the loyalty of my friendship to them." Ironic how their means of testing my loyalty to our friendship was to cut off all communication with me randomly at recess. If only the problems in a twenty-year-old's world today were the same as when we were in third grade.

I did learn a very important lesson that day, though: the value of forgiveness. They could tell I was upset, and you'd better believe I was very upset. I was angry, sad, frustrated, and confused, all at the same time. *Why the heck don't they want to talk to me? What did I do wrong?* All those tormenting thoughts—just to find out it was a test? Thanks, but no thanks, or as my girl Ariana Grande says, "Thank you, *next.*" The only tests I could handle at that point in my life were those in my phonics class, not in my relationships. However, I clearly remember thinking, *If I don't forgive them, I'll lose them forever.*

Even at a young age, we see that it is an unnatural feeling to forgive. We don't necessarily want to do it. We don't want to give someone the key to the door out of feeling bad for their mistakes. We want them to hurt the way they hurt us. Am I right? We want them to feel guilty, shameful, pained, and bruised, just as they caused us to feel, because we live in a society where "justice" is proposed as the basis of equality. Yet forgiveness doesn't act like that. Forgiveness isn't a "you did me wrong, I'll do you wrong, and then we're even" sort of concept. Sometimes forgiveness involves trading in our pain, insecurity, and projection of vulnerability for love and peace.

I knew even in third grade that I absolutely 100 percent did not want to forgive my friends. They were so mean to me, leaving me out of recess … for God's sake, they didn't even ask me to go make mud cakes with them that day, the nerve! That stirred a fire in me, and I wanted them to feel the burn of it. Scratch that; I wanted them to get *stung* by the burn of. It was not a natural feeling for me to want to forgive them. However, even in third grade where self-development concepts were nowhere near my awareness, let alone expertise, there was something natural in me that knew if I didn't find peace with the situation—of course after talking to them about how wrong it was and how much it hurt me—I would lose some friendships that meant a lot to me.

Forgiveness is like an investment. It is letting go of the right now, even if it is hard and painful, to invest in a future that is free from the captivity to a grudge. To repeat, *forgiveness is not natural.* It is something we choose to do even if it is hard. Here's the thing, though: forgiveness, as selfless and other-centered as it may seem, is totally for self-benefit. When you forgive somebody, you are doing it for you. Carrying around the pain from what someone else has done to you is like carrying them around on your back for the rest of your life. Holding that grudge does not make the other person keep feeling bad; it does not make them feel any less as a person, and it does not decrease their humanity, stature, or reputation. In fact, the only thing holding a grudge against someone does is tear *you* down. It eats you from the inside out. A wise man once said it is like putting poison into your own body yet hoping your enemy is the one who dies.

Refusing to forgive someone else for their wrongdoings to you only brings you down; it does not bring them down too. Here's the reality, the one that you probably don't want to hear: they're going to get over it. No matter how much you torment them, how much hate you keep in your heart, no matter what bad juju you send their way, they will get over it at some point. Will you get over it, though? My friends were going to get over leaving me out of recess that one day. In fact, even if I didn't forgive them, they probably still would've stopped feeling bad about it before the end of that day. (Granted, we were in third grade, a time when our emotional capacity was about the size of a mustard seed, so huge emotional drama spills lasted about one minute and the aftereffects probably less than that.)

My point is, when you refuse to allow forgiveness into your life and into the wounds other people have caused from their wrongdoings, you only allow those wounds to grow more and more infected. It is like not putting ointment onto the wound: it will either (1) grow more infected, (2) just sit there as it is, not getting worse but not getting better, or (3) take an exponentially longer time to heal than it would if you cleaned it. You must release yourself from that cage. You must *let go* to grow. Holding on to grudges, old flames, past wrongdoings, even pure evil done to you, is only going to infect your wounds more or make them take longer to heal.

Release. Let go. Do this by identifying why what that person did to you touches you in a place so deeply that it's hard for you to let go of. Why is that cut the person drew, so deep in you? Perhaps it evoked an underlying fear or insecurity. For most people who can't seem to forgive someone for a wrong done to them, that action touched a wound that was already there. Let's say your ex-girlfriend cheated on you with your best friend a few years ago, and you still haven't been able to let it go. Was what she did horrible? Absolutely. However, I guarantee that—after a few years of still holding on the grudge, hatred, anxiety, and rage—the pain of her cheating on you probably had more to do with you than her. Her disloyalty touched something in you, an underlying fear of never being good enough in the first place. The fact that she cheated on you with your best friend validated (in your mind) that you weren't in fact good enough. You cannot forgive her because you cannot let go of that wound you have always held. If you addressed that deep insecurity in you, you'd be much more able to let go of and forgive the past situation; you would free yourself from a lot of built-up tension and could start living a more peaceful life from that point.

Identify your underlying issues. That is where all hesitation and failure to forgive starts. Get to know your own wounds until they are second nature to you. This will allow you to understand why it is so hard for you to forgive someone for certain things. Have you ever wondered why for some things it's easy as pie to forgive someone, yet for certain things it'd actually be the equivalent of moving a mountain for you to forgive them? That's because it is all dependent on your underlying insecurities. Not only do the people who harm us do this through projecting their insecurities onto us, but we also project our deepest insecurities onto other people by refusing to forgive them. Don't let yourself fall into that trap and end up living a life with tons of extra weight on your back from the grudges you are carrying.

Do this exercise. I call it the unclothing exercise. I want you to get naked! Absolutely, undeniably, unequivocally naked. Stop taking your clothes off! Dirty-minded people! I mean I want you to get *emotionally* naked. I want all masks off, all coping mechanisms stopped, and all fears and overlying compensations made visible. I want you to be raw and real, ladies and gents. Sit down and start listing big things in your life you think you still carry the weight of on your heart. That girl who broke your heart four years ago? That boss who let you go? Your parents who were never around much and then skipped your college graduation for a vacation in Bali? Write it out. All the stuff, let it out.

Get so naked with your emotions that you truly feel as if you have squeezed out every last ounce of tension weighing down the magic in your heart. Once you've written it out, I want you to go through and write down potentially why you had the reaction you did when that event happened. When your boyfriend broke up with you, did you wall up and swear off love (writing from experience here) because his breaking up with you touched your already existing wound of never feeling good enough? That rumor about yourself you heard the girls in your sorority exchanging after Greek Week, did it hurt you because of what they actually said? Or was it because it touched the people-pleaser wound in you that if everyone doesn't like you then your worth is nothing?

Identify the painful situations having a grip on your life at the moment. Usually these painful events have a common underlying pattern as to why they hurt you in the way they do. For me I see the theme of "not being good enough" popping up time and time again. Each time a guy broke up with me, a coach didn't play me, a boss let me go, an internship didn't hire me, my mom got mad at me, I got a bad grade, girls were gossiping about me … they all hit this wound of not being smart enough, pretty enough, athletic enough, competent enough, etc., time and time again. Once I realized it wasn't the external situations dictating the insecurities that popped up after they happened but instead how the external situations hit on a wound that had always been *deep inside me*, I realized that if I confronted that internal wound, I could change how I perceived the situations. Now, when situations like that occur, I know it isn't the situation that is making me upset, but my internal wound. For me personally, I remind myself of my worth in the mirror. I say to myself when I am feeling insecure, "I have so much love within myself that I do not have to change myself or prove to anyone that I'm good enough to receive love from other people." This brings me back to center and personal abundance.

Unforgiving people live unfulfilled lives; hate, anger, and frustration feed their hearts and actions. They fall into the "victim" mind-set of "Why did this happen to *me*? What did I do to deserve this?" Now I am not saying the next time your best friend steals a quarter of a million dollars from you, go forgive them right off the bat, and continue your friendship with them. You must absolutely feel the pain, hurt, rage, and sadness that come when others deceive you. What I *am* saying is this: when you are deceived, use the opportunity as a way to shine light on some of your insecurities. "Why is it so hard for me to forgive this person? What wound of mine did they touch that is causing me so much resistance to letting go of this situation?" Earlier I mentioned the "WTOH—What's the opportunity here?" rule; implement that in these situations. Learn from these situations.

Practice forgiveness because as noted earlier, it is not natural. Understand that sometimes forgiveness may look like getting some distance from previous relationships. Use the example mentioned earlier, in which a best friend did something very deceitful toward you. You do not have to continue being their greatest friend in the world; in fact, I strongly encourage you against it, depending on the situation. Trust was broken; that will take time to mend, and sometimes it never does mend.

Forgiveness does not mean going on your merry way, pretending nothing happened. It simply means letting go of the situation so it doesn't weigh heavily on you any longer. Forgive your friend after feeling the pain you're going to feel. Let go. Move on, but know that moving on for you may not include that friendship any longer, and that is okay. Through each troublesome experience, we grow and we change. We morph into someone different from the person we were before that experience. This new you may not look like the same person who could uphold that same friendship as earlier. Embrace this new you. Grow into the newest and greatest version of yourself, using this experience as an opportunity to identify wounds in you that you didn't even know were there. Let go of the hateful experience. Forgive.

Forgiveness isn't just about others. Sure, others will do things that hurt us, break us down, tear us apart, maybe even shake us to our core. However, if I asked a hundred people who their biggest critic was, I bet ninety-nine would say themselves. We are constantly bashing on ourselves, am I right? We go through our days getting irritated with ourselves when we do even the smallest of things like go up the wrong staircase, call the wrong person, drop our phone, make the wrong turn—this list might never end.

I know you know what I'm talking about. I distinctly remember turning right instead of going straight one time on the way to tennis practice, and you would've thought I'd just burned down the White House by accident. I was tearing myself apart with my words. *I had simply gone the wrong way at a stop sign. I did not cause world hunger or a deadly disease, set the Amazon on fire, melt all the ice in the Arctic* ... nope, nothing that extreme at all. I just took a route about three minutes longer than usual to get to tennis.

What is that? What is all this built-up angst we have in ourselves? It comes from writing off difficult situations we are experiencing instead of thinking through how we can grow from them. It results from all the many occasions, large or trivial, when we did not forgive ourselves. That's why little things can trigger Godzilla in us to come out.

I've told you how, when I was younger, I struggled with body image and self-love. I did not love myself. From the outside looking in, it seemed as if I had the most confidence one could possibly have. I was happy, assured, bubbly, and loving on other people; but this love on others never translated to self-love for me. On the inside I was broken.

I became hyper aware of what I looked like on the outside. This was an extremely poor mind-set to have, especially during the time of ... the hair crisis. The summer before my sophomore year of high school I had decided to get with the latest trend of being blonde. Everyone loved blondes— and by everyone, I mean boys loved blondes. I wanted to be blonde so incredibly bad; like I said, I was hyper aware of my physical appearance.

I used a product that supposedly would give you that "natural, beachy, sun-kissed" blonde. Let me tell you, all it did was make my hair legit orange. I was a mix between a blonde-, orange-, red-, and brown-haired girl. Super sexy, I know. Thing was, the "blonde" part of my hair was at the very top of my head, the area that surrounds my face, so it was the only thing I could see. So naturally, because I couldn't see the pumpkin orange and hot tamale red coloring on the backside of my head, I thought I looked *damn* good.

My mother begged to differ, and after much arguing, I finally caved in and agreed to have it professionally dyed back to normal (which is light brown). Thing was, my mom didn't come to this hair appointment, so I decided to get a little sneaky and asked the woman to dye it all blonde. Oh boy, did she do the job. My hair was blonde all right, but not your silky, honey, sun-kissed, fresh beach look blonde; you know the blonde I'm talking about—think Blake Lively or Kate Hudson. Yeah, no.

This blonde was the *white* blonde. I mean *snow white* blonde. I know silver is all in right now, but let me tell you, back then it wasn't, and even if it was, I could never pull it off. I resembled what I think my grandmama Janet's colored hair would look like if she didn't dye it: white. I was devastated, horrified, and actually felt sick to my stomach. I went back day after day for the following week trying to fix it, but all this did was kill my hair (and heart) each time they tried to "fix" it and couldn't. Finally I went to another lady who said she could fix it. She did a "honey" glaze, and I looked in the mirror to see *red* hair. I mean, *red*. Round two of absolute devastation ensued.

Now why am I telling you all this? Why am I divulging the story of all this devastation and pain? Because at this time I put everything into my physical appearance, and when I was suddenly well below satisfied with how I looked, I absolutely hated myself. Mentally, I abused myself. I said the worst of things to myself every single day this was going on. I genuinely loathed who I was and refused to allow myself to see that "ugly creature" in the mirror.

I also hurt myself. In the bathroom one night I was so desperate to have something to take my mind off my hair and the horrible feeling of worthlessness that consumed me from the inside out, I punched myself in the face. I figured, *If I can't drown out the pain I'm feeling, I just need another sort of pain to put my focus on.* I socked myself smack in my right eyeball. It didn't leave a nasty bruise, only a little discoloring. When people asked,

I told them someone hit me with a ball when I was at the net playing a doubles tennis match. Word of advice: actively creating more pain in your life to distract yourself from the pain you're already feeling doesn't do anything but cause you more pain.

I never forgave myself for this until this very year. This had been something that I felt ashamed of, something to hide. Yes, my hair grew out, and yes, I finally started getting correct highlights (God bless). But regardless, the internal scars from my mental and physical abuse had never "grown out." They were always still there, just under the surface. Because I'm someone who promotes self-love, positivity, and joy, all day every day, I felt this was something I could never share, because I would be deemed a hypocrite. So I buried it, acting as if it never happened. I could still promote happiness and positivity but never deal with the parts of my past where I did not personally feel those things, right? Wrong. Time and time again when I talked to someone who wasn't loving themselves fully, I found that I could listen to them and talk with them, telling them that just because they are where they are right now doesn't mean they'll be here forever; all they need is time and forgiveness. But afterward, part of me left those meaningful conversations with the feeling that there was still work left undone. That thing was forgiving myself for what *I* had done to me years earlier.

Forgive yourself. Let go of the things that capture your heart in a cage and prevent it from being shown to the world. You have scars, visible and invisible, that have caused you pain, damage, heartbreak, and hurt. However, those scars have also molded you into the person you are today. They have shaped you, changed you, grown you into the masterpiece you are right now. Without scars you have no stories to tell, no reliability to project to others, and no opportunities for growth to go through.

I hurt myself. I said horrible and nasty things to myself. I put myself down. I hit and punched myself. I starved myself. I pulled my hair. I screamed at myself. The list could go on for a while. However, I am also standing here today, writing this book to you guys. Without those experiences, I would not have it in me to write this book, to connect with the people I do each day, or to tell my story.

Forgiving yourself is brave. It is not easy and does not come naturally. However, it is absolutely necessary to use the hardships and hurts we have caused to ourselves as stepping-stones of growth in our lives. The only way to transform these hardships, these stones weighing you down, into stepping-stones is to release the guilt and shame you cloak them in, forgive yourself, and let go. By forgiving yourself, you provide yourself with the opportunity to learn from your past mistakes, making your future stronger than it would have been without those mistakes in the past. You are a living, walking miracle. Let go of the grudges you hold against yourself for your past mistakes, and use them instead as the fuel for your rocket ship which will propel you to a life better than the life you'd be living without those mistakes.

TAKE NOTE:

1. Forgiveness is not just for other people; it is for you. Letting go of any grudges you are holding toward others frees you from a lifetime of the shackles in which grudges can imprison you.

2. Usually it isn't the act of someone treating us unjustly that causes us to be upset. It is how that act hits on internal wounds we've had for a while. Once you address these wounds, you develop a discipline that allows you to determine how you are going to react to situations that once would have torn you apart. Write down situations that have taken a heavy toll on your emotions and your heart. Then write down what internal wound these circumstances could be hitting on. Are you afraid of commitment? Is your biggest fear being alone? Maybe you're like me, and the fear of not being good enough is buried deep down there. It's going to take a lot of digging and searching to figure it out, but trust me, it is there. Get naked with yourself. Get raw and real. Put down your mask.

3. Remember that in order to truly be our best selves, we must forgive ourselves for our own mistakes; Lord knows we've got them. Holding a grudge against yourself prevents you from growing in any way, shape, or form from the incident. *You did what you did.* It's done, no changing it. The best way to go from here is to take it and learn how to grow from it. To do that, you must first forgive yourself.

4. I took this exercise from Lisa Nichols, a well-known self-development speaker and author. It worked wonders in my life. Every morning, looking in the mirror, I say to myself seven things I forgive myself for. I look myself dead in the eyes, after my 4:30 a.m. cup of coffee, and repeat seven things I am truly ready to release from having any weight on my heart any longer. These things are sometimes simple, like not responding to that girl's text asking me to dinner … from two weeks ago. Sometimes they're bigger, like not being honest with my mom about how I truly felt when she yelled at me or being mean to myself the other day when I didn't like the way my body looked in the mirror. Sometimes it has to do with my past, like forgiving myself for guarding my heart from anyone and everyone after my first boyfriend broke up with me. Say these seven things to yourself in the mirror. Make them count, and make them hold emotional value to you. Over time you will see any grudges slowly start to loosen their grip.

CHAPTER 20

Be Your Own FOMO

FOMO: the fear of missing out. It eats us all alive. You know exactly what I'm talking about. You're at home on a Saturday night in your rainbow-colored fuzzy slippers and the oversized T-shirt that you stole from your dad's closet, binge-watching *The Office*, and you wander on to your Snapchat or Instagram stories just to see your friends or a group of people you hardly know at some raging party without you. Your mind instantly starts to go in a million directions on how much fun they're having without you, how much your life sucks compared to theirs, how much you wish you were there, blah-blah-blah.

It is tormenting when our minds go on this continuous loop, like a broken record, with these thoughts of how since we're are not at that party, concert, birthday dinner, or whatever, our lives must suck, and we have no reason to be happy with where we are in the moment. Crazy sounding? Absolutely. Does this happen all the time? You bet.

I remember one specific time in high school, I traveled with a group of students to Ecuador, where my high school owned a piece of property, to study there for two weeks. Not gonna lie; it was hands down one of the best trips of my life. It was the most amazing group of people in the most amazing place. At the time I was still dating my first boyfriend, who was not on that trip. For ten days we were on the property that my high school owned with no service. Then the day before we flew home, we stayed in Quito, Ecuador's capital. When I finally got service back, of course first thing I did was text my boyfriend. I eventually got around to texting my parents, friends, and siblings too to let them know I was alive and hadn't died getting attacked by a mountain lion on any hikes or anything like that, but priorities were first: got to text my boyfriend. When we finally could text each other I found out he was going to a concert that night with some of our high school friends.

I don't know about you guys, but when I was in high school (a total of three years ago), concerts seemed to be what everyone did. Maybe this was just an Atlanta thing, or even just a thing my friend group did, but we all went to concerts to hang out. I knew people who went to several concerts a week, and on school nights! Sheesh, to someone who's literally in bed by 10:30 and considers staying up till midnight her idea of "rallying," those people were hardcore.

So my boyfriend at the time was going to this concert, where I knew there were going to be drunk girls, drunk guys, crazy music, blurred lights, and touchy dancing, and he himself would most likely be drunk. All of a sudden, even as I was coming off this high from a week of indescribable scenery, amazing new friendships, a new appreciation for a different culture, and too many sewed headband souvenirs to count, I had a pit in my stomach the size of Texas. There I was in this beautiful city, a place with so much liveliness, richness, and culture surrounding me at every glance, and all I could think about was how much I wanted to be at that sweaty, dirty, headache-provoking techno concert with my boyfriend because (1) I wanted to spend time with him, (2) I didn't want any girl trying to pull a fast one, and (3) I didn't want his intoxicated self pulling a fast one on any other girl.

It consumed me. I had so much fear of missing out on that concert, which I couldn't possibly get to, that I missed out on embracing the magic of a city I may never see again for the rest of my life. I was surrounded by incredible people, breathtaking views, and magnificent culture, yet my mind was anywhere but there. I missed out on an incredible memory because I couldn't appreciate where I was in the moment; instead I was thinking about where I wasn't.

What if we truly believed, with every ounce of our being, that where we are in this very moment is exactly where we need to be in life? What if we felt the magic of the fact that for some reason out of all the places we could be, things we could be doing, people we could be with, surroundings we could be seeing, and magic we could be feeling, our body, heart, and soul were put here (wherever here is for you) in this moment? Don't you think that would make you look at the very moment you're living with a little more appreciation, magic, curiosity, and gratitude?

What if we could be our own FOMO? Instead of looking at Snapchat stories, Instagram stories, Twitter, Facebook, and the rest, seeing what everyone else is doing and comparing it to our own lives just to conclude that everyone else's life is so much better than our own, what if we truly felt in our bones that wherever we are in this moment is where we are meant to be? What if we feared missing out on the moment *we* are living right now, not the moment everyone else is living? What if in each and every moment, whether we are at that amazing party or not, we looked around and took it for what it is: an opportunity to be feel the magic of this living second?

There is some reason you are where you are right now. No, you may not be at that party, and all your friends may be. No, you may not be in the Bahamas for spring break like all your friends are, while you are having to go on college tours. No, you may not have your life all figured out or have gotten that job offer like everyone else seems to have already gotten, but where you are in this very second is exactly where you need to be. Something out there, whatever you believe—God, the universe, or some mystical power greater than us—aligned your soul, heart, body, and spirit to be in this very place at this very time with these very people, feeling this very way for a reason.

Look around. Embrace it. Have fear of missing out on the moment you are living right now, not the moment your friends, boyfriend, girlfriend, parents, teammates, or spouse is living. Embrace every last spec of this moment—from those as big as everything you can see, to the specs as little as the very breaths that fill your lungs and the feelings that are flooding your heart.

Fear missing out on *your* moment. Fear missing out on your surroundings, your opportunity to connect with what's around you right now, your path of life that is being created for you, by living this very moment to its fullest. Don't look at others and think wherever they are in life is where you need to be, because it is not. Their moments are their moments to live, not yours. If I had implemented this years ago when I was in Ecuador worrying about missing out on a Flux concert with my boyfriend, instead of having tainted memories of anxiety and worry, I'd have memories of deep connection with the incredible people, culture, and life bursting around me.

Every single day of my life since I've learned this lesson, I deeply fear not being present wherever I am at in that moment. I don't want to miss out on a connection with someone, a thought I could be thinking, a feeling I could be feeling, or any other opportunity to grow myself and lead myself toward the life I want to cultivate. Be your own FOMO. Fear missing out on the very moment your body, soul, spirit, and heart have aligned themselves to be at right now.

TAKE NOTE:

1. When you feel that ball of anxiety creep up as you spot that Snapchat story, Instagram highlight, Facebook photo, or tweet, I literally want you to say out loud, preferably to yourself in a mirror, "Pause." Pause the situation. Do not let your mind spiral out of control into thinking sinkholes as to why their life is so much better than yours, why they must hate you because you weren't invited, why they are prettier or skinnier or tanner or better than you—just pause it! Pause the chatter! If you can interrupt the thought, you can stop the thought pattern from creeping in.

2. After you pause the thought, repeat "I do not receive that." Don't receive it! Stop it from penetrating into your mind! Immediately look for the magic of this moment. Are you at home watching Netflix? You go, girl! Get yourself a fir tree candle, light that thing up, pop some popcorn (and if you're like me, you'll put some Skittles in it), and luxuriate in the fact you are rocking the self-care game tonight. You're at a conference for work while all your friends are at that party? Focus on the relationships you could build at the conference; you never know what friendships might arise. Or focus on defining yourself as a committed, kickass leader at this conference.

3. There is always a reason you are where you are. Look for it. Ask yourself, "What can I be looking at that will give me a sign as to why I am here in this moment right now?"

CHAPTER 21

Be Your Own Safe Zone

If you've lived long enough, I hope you've had at least one moment of absolute freedom to be, do, say, act, and feel however you wish. A moment when the world's opinions of you washed away, and you laughed, danced, sang, shouted, or loved in a way that was completely carefree.

A moment like this happened for me about a month and a half ago at something called the band party at my college, Wofford, the Saturday night before the first classes of my junior year. For the past two years I've been on Orientation staff for Wofford, welcoming all the first-year students into our special home and pounding them for a week with group activities, icebreakers, "get to know you" games, field day competitions, and Camp Greystone day trips.

Most incoming first-years totally hate this stuff, but we O-staffers (the peeps running the show) live for this week. It's a chance for all the clique barriers to completely break down between us. You have baseball players and fraternity brothers dancing their asses off together to T-Pain's "Buy You a Drank"; you have campus union delegates and soccer stars battling it out in the game Ninja Star; you have students of all majors, all backgrounds, all hobbies, all interests, and all activities coming together for one simple goal—to make sure these first-year students feel as comfortable as possible being themselves in their new home. It is truly a week to be as weird, as freakish, and as you as possible.

There was one moment at the band party that Saturday night when it just hit me: *This is what being me truly feels like.* The liberation of being myself, not worrying about people looking at me, how they were looking at me, or why they were looking at me, filled my soul. The band was playing "Finesse" by Bruno Mars (I am a complete Bruno Mars fan girl; by the way—Bruno, if you ever read this, it is my life goal to meet you, but no pressure), and I was at the very front dancing my tail off. I was shaking my body in such a way that one would've thought I was possessed, but I did not care. I danced the way my body was wanting to dance. I sang at the top of my lungs. I shimmied my tail feather as hard as I could and completely by myself. None of my closest friends were around to cloak myself in. I was up there dancing on my own.

The best part was when I got to get up on stage. The band was taking a quick water break, and I got up there and requested my all-time favorite song, "Bed Rock." Why is this my favorite song? you might ask. Only because I know every stinkin' tootin' word! I can rap that sucker in my sleep. It's my go-to party trick. A party needs to be pumped up a little? No problem, just turn on "Bed Rock," and I'll get that thing going.

In the past, thoughts would've flooded my mind with *Oh my god, people are looking at me. I need to make sure my dance moves are the coolest, smoothest, and chicest things out there for this.* Or *Oh my god, do I look skinny enough? I am so sweaty right now, are people going to think I'm disgusting?* But not this time.

This time all I did was focus on this incredible moment. Here I was on stage, with two other amazing people on O-staff, in front of Wofford just singing "Bed Rock" at the top of our lungs, not giving a fly whether our dance moves were "cool" or even with the beat. We weren't worrying about whether our outfits looked right, whether our sweat dripping onto people right up near the stage grossed everyone out (which it totally did; I mean, c'mon, it grossed *me* out, and I wasn't the one getting dripped on), or whether anyone thought we were obnoxious getting up there taking over the stage. Nope, the only thing we were focused on was how much damn fun we were having and how free we felt to completely be ourselves.

I had that moment—that moment where I was completely liberated to be whoever I wanted to be. Let me tell you, it felt so freakin' good. It got me thinking, why is it that just for one week I was allowing myself to be as weird as possible? Just for orientation week I was letting myself be free to be? Initially it was because I figured that if I let myself be as free as possible to be me, then it would inspire the incoming freshmen to truly let themselves be free to be them. Thing is, it felt so good to just not care, not worry, not consume my thoughts with the question of how other people are perceiving what I am doing.

This is what I learned that week: Our fear of someone else judging us is birthed from the pain we self-inflict by first creating our own judgments on our actions, feelings, thoughts, or appearance. We judge ourselves before anyone else can. It is that pain from our own judgments that either (1) allows us to create this idea in our mind that everyone else is judging us in exactly the same way we are judging ourselves or (2) allows our personal judgments to open the gateway for people's actual judgments to seep into our minds and affect us. If we can stop judging ourselves, then the fear of others judging us will end too.

Think about it. Say, for example, you're having a really hard time being vulnerable with your new boyfriend about your feelings. Every time he talks to that girl, you get this knot in your stomach because you know they have a history or that he liked her before, and you're just not comfortable with it. Thing is, no matter how hard you try, you just cannot seem to open up to your partner about how you are feeling about this. Every time you try, you seem to freeze up and convince yourself it isn't that big a deal. That is your already predetermined judgments on your feelings writing a story for how you think your partner is going to judge you. You have judged your thoughts as unnecessary, ridiculous, or crazy, and that judgment you have created for yourself is telling you that your partner is going to judge you that way too. Thing is, *you haven't even talked to your partner about it.* You have no idea whether that's how they will react. But because you judged yourself that way, you figure they will too.

Our judgments of ourselves dictate how we feel others will judge us. You want to wear that bright yellow polka-dot outfit? You judge it to be too much, so you fear others will also think it's too much, so you don't wear it. That bright pink eyeshadow? Same thing. You think it is way too pink, so you automatically assume everyone else will too and don't put it on. If we can be our own safe zone—a zone of zero criticism—then we can stop our own judgments and thus stop our fear of everyone else's judgment.

When I was on that stage at the band party, I was not judging myself. I danced in the most ridiculous ways—shaking every body part, moving in all directions. Literally, at one point I was doing a move that was a cross between jazz hands and the classic "I'm underwater" arm wiggle. But because I wasn't judging myself, I was not afraid of everyone else's judgments, and if anyone did have judgments, because I closed off my brain from receiving any judgments by not judging myself, their judgments couldn't affect me.

Another important side note: there is nothing more beautiful than those who are entirely, unapologetically themselves. If you can stop judging yourself, then you can stop that fear of others' judgments from kicking in. If you think you're doing awesome at life, then you naturally believe others think the same about you; and if they don't, it doesn't affect you! Because your brain has already accepted the belief that "I am doing awesome at life," so anything that doesn't agree with that belief is disregarded.

Whenever you feel yourself falling prey to others' judgments of you, ask yourself what you are judging about yourself in the moment. More likely than not, the thing you think everyone is judging you about, you have already judged yourself for first. If you can identify that internal judgment and release it, you may simultaneously find that your perception of others' judgments releases too. Identify the judgment you are making, and replace it with an uplifting power statement.

Do you fear that someone is judging you for the way your face turns really red when you give presentations? Replace the degrading thought you already have about yourself that says, "I'm so awkward, I make people uncomfortable when I speak in front of them," or "no one cares about what I am saying," with powerful statements such as "I blush because I get so passionate about my presentation topic. I am wonderfully and powerfully made and am capable of bringing such energy to this presentation that it captivates my audience," or "I am one hell of a badass and can connect with any audience you put me in front of." Interrupt the degrading and judgmental conversation you are having with yourself.

The truth is that no one judges you as much as you judge yourself. Why? Because that would require devoting a lot of their time and energy to you. People don't do that. They have their own lives to worry about. They aren't going to waste 99 percent or even 25 percent of it on judging you! So when it comes to judgment, you need to start combating the right opponent—yourself. You are your ultimate judger.

Rewrite the judgmental thoughts in your head. Be your own safe zone.

Do not judge yourself, whether it's about something you want to wear, a dance move you're jiving to, a polka-dot bandana you really want to wear, a bright purple lipstick you feel compelled to paint on, or an emotion that is consuming you. You feel jealous? That's a part of life; no judgment. Dive deep into why you feel jealous, maybe talk to someone about it, and use it to grow. Do not judge yourself. Once you judge yourself for feeling a certain way, you prevent yourself from talking to others about it and gaining insight because you fear they already judge you in the same way you are judging yourself.

Allow yourself to do as you wish, feel as you please, say what is on your mind, and live the way you want to live. Be your own safe zone—a zone of no judgment.

TAKE NOTE:

1. You are the dictator of the judgmental conversation you have been playing in your head for years and years.
2. When you find yourself worried about the judgments of others, pause the worry spiral conversation you are having in your head. Are others really judging you for that? Or are you judging yourself first?
3. Rewrite a judgmental thought about yourself with a power statement: "I am capable of communicating to this audience with excellent energy and abundant radiance." "I am the most fun, carefree light of life out here on the dance floor and don't need anyone or anything but the music and my dancing shoes out here with me to have a good time." "I love my new bright pink hair because it symbolizes my boldness, daring, and ability to try new things." *Interrupt your judgment conversation.* Once you do, I promise that you'll find you become less bothered by others' judgments, and your own will lessen in volume in your life.

CHAPTER 22

Be Your Own Growth

So I'm talking to this guy right now. Talking, dating, hanging out—I really can't keep up with what society labels people who are in that "in between" phase. I mean, could society nowadays make the guidelines of dating any more confusing? I wish there were a handbook called *How to Have a Healthy "Thing" with Someone*. Not a healthy relationship or marriage, 'cause God knows we're not there yet; nope, just how to have a healthy "thing" with someone because that seems to be what everyone has with other people if they are not blissfully in love and declared to be boyfriend and girlfriend.

In my past relationships I've really struggled with how to explicitly say what I am feeling. This is totally the people pleaser in me- I don't want to say something that'll make them feel uncomfortable or think that I am crazy in the noggin. If I am jealous, upset, uncomfortable, or confused, I'll usually just keep it to myself. I won't say anything about it unless they pry it out of me, because I'm afraid of making them uncomfortable, since if they're uncomfortable, I'm uncomfortable.

Thing is, that's not how successful relationships function. You have to be able to explicitly say how you are feeling in order for the relationship and yourself to grow.

With the guy I am talking to now, I am trying something brand-new. I am trying to be okay with being uncomfortable. When I feel something, I say it—even if it's something that I've never thought I'd be able to say out loud to someone I was dating, something like instigating sexual conversations or curiosities. I push myself to ask those questions, say those statements, and stir that conversation.

I've learned that the more I put myself in discomfort, the more comfortable I become over time with whatever made me uncomfortable in the first place. Ironically, it is only by putting ourselves through the uncertainty that we can gain insight into the most certain revelation: it is in times of our greatest discomfort that we open ourselves up to the opportunity to grow.

I know it's scary. Whatever it is for you—buying that new car, moving to another state, breaking up with that boyfriend, having that serious "defining the relationship" conversation for the first time. I know it makes your stomach go into knots, twists, and turns that you didn't even think were possible, but let those cues be your road signs that you're going the right way. If your body is physically telling you that you are uncomfortable, keep on going, because you're growing.

Do you remember growing pains? For some of you it might've been decades ago, for some of you, it might not have been too long ago. Growing pains suck. I remember tossing and turning at night because my legs were totally uncomfortable, and no matter how much I shook or massaged or slapped them, the pain wouldn't leave them alone. Now think back to when the pain stopped. Did you wake up the next morning, and suddenly you were like, *"Holy cow! I got so much taller!"*? Absolutely not, unless it was some monumental, world-record growth spurt that has yet to be recorded in the *Guinness Book of World Records*. However, give it some time, and it will be noticeable that you have gotten taller, even if you can't see if right off the bat. That's why that happens when you go to Thanksgiving brunch and all your relatives look at you in astonishment because you've grown so much (and you're just thinking, *What was her name again?*). You yourself don't notice your growth because it is subtle, and you are always with yourself so you cannot detect the change; however, it is noticeable to other people because even though your growth is occurring little by little, you are in fact growing.

That is exactly how we grow in our mentality and personal development as well. It doesn't happen overnight, and sometimes even after putting ourselves through one difficult situation after another, constantly taking on uncomfortable situations, we still may not see anything change; but it *is* changing. You are growing. Each time you feel uncomfortable and your stomach goes into knots, your palms sweat, your heart rate picks up, and you feel squeamish and unsure, those are your growing pains right there. Those are not signs to run away, hide, or fall back on your crutch. No! Those are your growing pains, pushing you further and further on your growth spurt toward personal mastery. Discomfort is a prerequisite for growth. If you are not uncomfortable, you are not growing.

Every morning one of my affirmations is "I live for being uncomfortable. It is only in my discomfort that I can grow. How will I grow today?" Then I sit and reflect on all the things I can do to put myself in a growth situation. Who's that person I'm afraid to talk to or that thing I'm afraid to talk about? What's that thing I'm afraid to do? I identify it and then decide it is time to put myself in the discomfort of my fear and take it on. I get nervous, my stomach goes into knots, my knees shake, sometimes I can't feel my legs—but guess what, those are my growing pains.

Unlike your actual growing pains that make you lankier, longer, and taller, you can have complete control over when your personal mastery growing pains happen. You can choose when you push yourself, rise up to uncomfortable occasions, and put yourself in situations that will instigate growth. Personal mastery growing pains are also unlimited, meaning there is no "maximum height" to be reached. You can grow as much as you push yourself to.

Unleash your growing pains. Even amid the uncertainty of the situation, you can be certain in your growth from rising up to the occasion and getting out of your comfort zone.

TAKE NOTE:

1. When you feel nervous, uncertain, shaky, wobbly, and afraid, take those cues as indications you are going in the right direction. You are going toward something that will bring you massive amounts of growth. How do I know this? Because if it didn't make you scared, that means it's something in your comfort zone. It's something you're already good at, not something that is going to push you or give you a new skill.

2. New skills only come through getting outside your comfort zone. Go in the direction of your fear. New skills, a greater understanding, personal development, and growth will develop in that pursuit.

CHAPTER 23

Be Your Own You

Let me totally pull the wool away from your eyes here for a second. In case you haven't realized this already, I am not a "professional" author by any means. If I have fooled you into thinking so, and this is heartbreaking news, I am dearly sorry, but in a way I'll quietly take it as a huge victory for myself.

Yes, I am writing this book; yes, I have drafted the pages, jotted down the stories, conveyed the lessons, and published this book. So at first glance it may look like I am very much an author by definition. Thing is, I never thought of myself as writing this book.

I'm only twenty! I'm in college. I don't have enough time to write a book or become an author. No, no—this is me simply putting fingers to keyboard on stories of mine and lessons I've learned that I don't want to forget. Right? Well, not quite.

I didn't think society could accept me as an author because (1) no one else around me at twenty years old is doing this, and (2) I was by no means the next Ernest Hemingway in any English class I have ever taken in my life—just your average gal trying to skate by with at least a B. But all that doesn't mean I couldn't be an author—and better yet even consider myself to be an author.

The reality is, though, that I am writing this book. I am an author who is telling her own story on to these pages. This isn't because I am the best writer in the world, craft the best sentences, have the best grammar, or even have the best story to tell; absolutely not. I am a writer because I feel it in my bones that I have a message to give to this world. That I have a purpose for putting these words on this page in hopes that it can even touch the heart of one person, in which case I will have done what I set out to do. I am a writer because my heart of passion is helping others become their greatest selves, and by doing this I can serve my passion to the world through the messages in this book.

That's the thing, y'all. Every one of you is unlike anyone else, yet at the same time you are like everyone else. Now before the part of you who heard from your parents that you were one of a kind and unlike anyone else starts having a panic attack, let me deconstruct this statement. Everyone on this planet is crafted into existence to serve ourselves, other people, and the earth itself, by the plan of whatever greater power you choose to believe—our Creator, the universe, some mystical force out there, whatever it is. I believe that our Creator made each and every one of us for one main purpose- to serve and love other people to our greatest ability and to honor Him by doing so. So in that regard, yes we are all just like everyone else in this world. We are all here for the same purpose: to serve.

However, how we choose to serve and how we are made to serve to our utmost ability is completely unique to each of us. A doctor and a lawyer both serve the greater good of humanity. They both help people every single day improve different areas of their lives and in many ways actually save lives on a consistent basis. Yet the doctor is not expressing her heart of service to the world by debating cases in courtrooms, and the lawyer is not giving his service to the world by holding a scalpel and performing operations in the ER. How the doctor and the lawyer act out their heart of service in this world is completely unique to them, making each of them unlike anyone else. Even how two different doctors interact with patients and families and go about doing their surgeries is entirely up to them individually. Once you realize that ...

(1) everyone has a purpose, meaning yes, *you have a purpose,*

(2) that purpose is to serve the greater good of humanity, and

(3) how you choose to carry out this purpose is appointed to everyone but chosen by *you,*

... you will start looking for the things that make you excel. It is when our heart, body, mind, and soul are aligned in our craft that we find our passion. Once we can learn how to use that passion in service to others, we have hit the jackpot. The world becomes this glittery, shiny, giant sparkle that consumes you from the inside out with its light once you have aligned your passion with service. That is when you can become your truest you—the you that was created to serve others and live out your passion, the you that was created in fact to use your passions to serve others. Align the purpose your Creator has given you- the opportunity to serve-, with the passion He has gifted to you, and you will find your own eternal bliss.

TAKE NOTE:

1. We are all placed here on this earth to serve. Period. Humanity grows and thrives when people are in harmony with the means by which they are serving the people in it.

2. Some people would argue their passion is to play Fortnite. I am not saying it isn't, but I will say that their Fortnite passion will not get them to a feeling of lifetime fulfillment. It is not serving anyone. (Some would argue with this, but the truth is pretty obvious.) Find that passion of yours that serves a greater purpose and feeds a greater cause. That is when you will find deep, raw, pure satisfaction for your life and the trajectory it is following.

3. Write down a list of your passions. What do you love to do? Do you love to fly kites? Ride bikes? Argue?

4. Now under each of those write down potential ways you could use those passions as means to serve a greater cause. Could you start a bike club at your college that organizes races and rides to go on throughout the year, giving people a community to turn to and encouragement to get active? If you like to argue, could you start pursuing your dreams of being a lawyer to give back to the community, or start a debate team at your school that allows others to have a space to speak up? It is good to be passionate about something, but use that passion, you guys! Unless it fuels some form of service, that passion is potential unexpressed. You can move mountains with passion as long as it is geared in a way that is of service to those on that mountain.

5. Pick just one of the passions you identified and dove into, and go for it. You may even do them all eventually, but take one at a time so your attention isn't scattered on multiple projects. This will ensure your entire focus is on that one goal, which increases the likelihood of it being successful.

CHAPTER 24

Be Your Own Hero

What can I say? I'm a dreamer. I love to dream about the future—anything and everything. When I was younger, I dreamed constantly about falling in love. I mean c'mon, what little girl didn't? We grew up with princess movies where Prince Charming swooped in and saved the day, and anything that was a problem beforehand was magically poofed away by a single kiss. The prince loved his princess no matter what her flaws were, even though in those movies it seemed they had none (even freaking animals followed their beautiful selves around everywhere they went).

I yearned for this as a little girl. I couldn't wait to meet my Prince Charming one day and have any fears, imperfections, or flaws that weighed heavy on my heart just disappear when he kissed me. As I got older, I wasn't necessarily picturing a Prince Charming, with the whole sword and outfit, but I definitely dreamed about that one guy who would fight for me no matter what, love me no matter what, and be there for me no matter what, and I dreamed of the moment he would say all that to me.

Yup, you may be thinking, *Oh my god, for real, Annie, c'mon,* but I know for a fact (man or woman reading this) that you dreamed about the same things. Why? Because that is the thing most strongly promoted by our society! Falling in love and finding the "right person" to fix all our problems is what our brains have been cultivated into dreaming about! Nearly all the TV shows, movies, songs, books, and plays revolve around love and how that "right person" is going to come along and fix everything that is broken in your life.

Here's a little secret, honey: it doesn't work like that. Despite what is promoted in society, *we* must be our own love story before we can possibly partake in a love story with someone else. *We* must fix our own problems before we can add someone else into the mix of crazy-ass lives. *We* must save ourselves before someone else can come in with their love.

Let me throw another little curveball of a thought at you. Amid all this dreaming for our desired Prince Charming (you know, the dreaming about how it would feel to fall in love with him, how we would meet, how we would treat him, how incredible it would feel to be so blissfully and hopelessly captivated by the force of that fairy-tale love), we forgot to dream about ourselves. Falling hopelessly in love with ourselves, dreaming about that moment we are blissfully and hopelessly in love with every single bit of us, thinking about how good it's going to feel the moment we finally throw in the towel and stop worrying about every single one of our imperfections and fall head over heels in love with us. Why is it that, growing up, instead we devote every ounce of our hopes and thoughts to this fairy-tale scenario of falling for Prince Charming? Why can't we be our own damn Prince Charming? Our own damn fairy tale? Fall for ourselves and then hope to one day fall for someone who builds us up higher than we could ever build ourselves alone? Why can't we be our own rescue, fairy tale, our dream come true—our own hero?

I'm not just talking about that perfect someone, either. For you, as a little kid or even now, what you dream about may not be finding that perfect person but instead finding that perfect achievement. You dream of winning that Oscar or Tony, publishing that book, or getting that promotion—and it is when you have achieved it that all your problems will be solved. Wrong! External circumstances—no matter whether it's a person, a sum of money, a promotion, an achievement, a move to the Bahamas—cannot save you from whatever problems or brokenness you are facing at the moment. Only you, every single beautiful, crooked, broken, shaken, strong part of you that is alive in this very moment, can save yourself from whatever you are facing.

You don't have to rely on external circumstances, people, or even "that perfect someone" to create the life you dream for yourself. You don't have to have these other "things" to feel free and in love with who you are. You can be your own hero right now, in this very moment. Accept who you are, what you have, and what you are capable of. Generate the feelings you wish to have about yourself and the characteristics your dream self would embody—and then choose to go be that right now. Once you reach a place in your life where you truly feel with every ounce of yourself that no matter what is happening around you, you will be able to save yourself and generate your own joy, confidence, and bliss, it is then that your relationships, business, health, and happiness will all skyrocket. Placing your ability to create your life and direct your destiny in your own hands prevents external circumstances from having any power over you.

Be your own hero. You can save your own self. You know you better than anyone else out there. You don't like who you are right now? Change it. You love who you are right now? Keep growing on that. Not all heroes have to wear capes—unless you want a cape; if so, then by all means *you do you,* and go for it. You don't have to be the hero who saves the world, but honey, you do need to be the hero who saves yourself. No one else is designed to do that job but you—not your husband, your girlfriend, your teacher, your coach, or your mom. Nope, none of them; you are.

I'll let you in on another little secret: by taking that first step to save yourself, in the long run you are acting as a hero of this world. By allowing yourself to be completely, entirely, and utterly you, you allow others to be completely, entirely, and utterly themselves. By giving off the contagious magic of what it truly means to be you into the world—and thus giving a fresh breath of air to a society that is tainted with fake profiles, misleading surnames, false résumés, and lies upon lies—you trigger a reaction of inspiring others to be their truest selves. That's pretty damn heroic if you ask me. You are saving the world from the suffering of one more villainous lie and deceitful mask that people throw on to "fit in" to society's standards. The world needs the truest form of you—with all the crooked, crazy, fun, loving, amazing, kick-ass parts of you! You can only truly let this part of you out to the world if you allow yourself to be your own hero when you feel your most vulnerable and scared. Go out, and shine your light; others will try to dim your light and throw massive shade on it, but be your own hero in these situations and protect your special sparkle. Remember, not just you, but the world needs your sparkle. Go shine it.

TAKE NOTE:

1. You have everything you need right now to make a change. I want you to really commit to going back and doing the practices in this book. Not because I told you so, not because the statistics say that's how you get the most benefit from self-development books, and not because you got peer pressured by the other members of your book club! Do the practices for you because that is how you will grow. You can have the nicest car in the world, but if you have no gas in the tank, then it will not go anywhere. This book can act as your car, but if you do not do the practices, that is like not putting gas in your tank. You will not grow. You must work your growth.

2. Affirm yourself every morning. It's been a year and four months now that I have not missed one morning of affirmations. The nerd in me could go into the phenomenon of how it promotes the rewiring of neural circuitry, but I won't bore you with those details. You guys, *it works.* I have at least three I say to myself every morning, and over the months they have changed, but these are mine as of right now-

    a. I have so much love within myself that I do not have to change me to get love from other people.
    b. Today I live for discomfort. It is only when I am uncomfortable that I am truly growing.
    c. I can do all things through Christ who strengthens me.

3. Find at least three affirmations you feel truly touch you from the inside out. I want you to feel each affirmation in your bones, nerves, and soul. Saying it should give you chills. Find something that you feel you truly need to work on, and rewrite the commentary in your head with an affirmation statement. I know that people-pleasing is a huge issue for me. I will go to lengths to change myself and my demeanor in order to make people more comfortable. That is why my first affirmation is one of them. I want to engrain in my brain, heart, and soul that on this day I will not change anything

about myself to get love from others. There's no need for that, since I already have such an overflow of love within me.

4. Put them everywhere. Tape them on your mirror, your desk, your laptop—display those affirmations! The more you see them, the more you say them, the stronger the connection and the more you will be reminded to embody them. Over time it will become second nature.

CHAPTER 25

Ta-Ta for Now

I've never been valedictorian, teacher's favorite, the most athletic, prettiest, or funniest person in the classroom. I haven't seen Mount Everest, the Great Wall of China, the Egyptian pyramids, or any other huge bucket-list landmark. I prefer taking naps on the floor rather than a couch or bed, I still get nervous before I raise my hand to ask a question in class, my go-to dance move is just jumping up and down as much as I can with my fists pumping in the air, and I get nervous at restaurants if I want to slightly change what side orders the menu specifies.

I wake up with horrible hair days when it looks like my curls have permanently taken on the identity of dreadlocks, I get zits from stressing too much about what's to happen in the future instead of focusing on the right now, and I will eat only fruity bubblegum, not minty. I am twenty years old, still in college, still fighting the urge to skip class at times, and if I'm in class, fighting the yawns that arise when I find the material absolutely irrelevant to my life.

Why am I saying all this? Because I want you to know I am human. I make mistakes; I have downfalls, struggles, and urges. I have days when I do feel I've implemented my rituals and habits and can easily conquer the temptations talked about in this book. Other days, I feel I am barely getting by, and if a gust of wind came at me, I would be carried away with it. It is in moments like those that the things talked about in this book will be the biggest source of light to you. The habits and rituals described will hold you accountable to acting as the best version of yourself, even if you don't feel that is possible.

No, I am not a valedictorian and never was the smartest person in my grade. In fact, when it came to writing, I struggled a lot in high school and still do in college. So what in the world made me decide to write a book? It was my story. Everyone has one, a story to tell from the life they have lived. I believe with my whole heart that I have experienced and learned things that all people need to hear—younger, middle-aged, older, male, or female. Have I learned it all? Absolutely not. Have I lived long enough to have a story to tell? Some may say no. However, it isn't their story to value or ignore; it is mine. All of you have a story to tell. How you tell it may not be through a book or novel, but instead by living out your passion and creating a lifestyle built off of your greatest desires.

The beautiful thing about our stories is that they're our own. We are the author of our own story. This means we can change it and alter it as we please. We can add to it, take from it, or completely erase and start all over. You have the choice right here and right now to write your own story and build the life you've always dreamed of. Reflect on who you are at this very moment, who you are surrounded with, where you are, what you are doing. Are you happy? Are you fulfilled? If you were to tell someone your story, would you be proud of the story you were telling?

You are your own story creator. Our lives are these big stories of everything we've gone through, learned about, grown from, and turned into. Think about your story, and go light the world up with it.

Sitting here in the Phase V market area of college, finally done editing the last chapter of this book, I feel the need for some major, creative, powerful send-off message. Still, I can truly say that the power of reading this book does not lie in this sentence but in the sentences on pages that fill this entire book. Hopefully, if I have done my job right, in reading it you have felt a fire continue to grow bigger and bigger in your belly, an emerging "I can" mentality and fortitude that grows and lights up every bit of your being.

I want you to know that you can. You always have been able to. Whatever it is you are going through, have been through, or are about to take on—you can. If you knew you couldn't fail, what dream would you let yourself dream? Why aren't you going after that dream now? You control you. You decide where you go and what you achieve.

You may not save the entire world, unless the next Gandhi or MLK is reading this right now, but you can save *your* world—the world you are living in and experiencing every single day. It all starts with ceasing to wait for some external validation to come into your life to rescue or energize you, and realizing you've had the power in you all along to save you. Save your dreams, your wishes, your sparkle, your magic ... save that little boy or that little girl that dreamed of dancing on stage, having their picture on the posters at Barnes & Noble, wearing the pantsuit with the briefcase. Save the magic in your heart that has always been there. Be the hero for yourself.

Annie Mayfield is a twenty-year-old lifestyle entrepreneur and author. She is currently a psychology major at Wofford College. At age nineteen she reached the top recognition rank in her health and wellness company one year after beginning her business. She gives multiple presentations a year on the importance of prioritizing physical, emotional, and mental health. In just one year she built and accumulated over sixteen thousand followers with her lifestyle Instagram account, using the media platform as a means to not only promote her business but also provide a large audience with entrepreneurial advice, marketing strategies, personal mastery skills, and lifestyle enhancers. Born and raised in Atlanta, Georgia, she now resides in Spartanburg, South Carolina, where she attends school.

CPSIA information can be obtained
at www.ICGtesting.com
Printed in the USA
LVHW080323300719
625691LV00018BA/1027/P